# STEP UP
## - AND -
# *Stand*
# OUT

*Fortune seeks the Brave*

# STEP UP
## - AND -
# *Stand*
# OUT

*Fortune seeks the Brave*

# DR DICKSON ALEROH

Published by Dr Dickson Aleroh. For all enquiries regarding both UK and international distribution, please, contact the publisher on +44 (0) 789-634-4244 or via email: info@dicksonaleroh.com. Alternatively, you can access our website, www.dicksonaleroh.com.

Cover created and designed by Fashion News Outlet | Fashion Magazine & P.R. - www.fnomagazine.com.

Printed in Great Britain

# Contents

# Introduction

*"Man often becomes what he believes himself to be. If I keep on saying to myself that I cannot do a certain thing, it is possible that I may end by really becoming incapable of doing it. On the contrary, if I have the belief that I can do it, I shall surely acquire the capacity to do it even if I may not have it at the beginning."*

*Mahatma Ghandi*

They say the journey of a thousand miles begins with a single step. Indeed, the compilation of this transformational, inspirational and motivational book has been an eye opener for me and I have learnt how to become one with myself through the conveyance and promulgation of my life experiences to the world. Hopefully, in centuries to come, by telling my story in the most succinct way I see fit, this generation, those before and those that are yet to be born, will all learn how to better themselves. No matter how insignificant you believe your story to be, there is a world out there waiting to hear, embrace and learn to better themselves from it. You are a beacon to the world and your Creator has purposed it to be so.

He has graciously gave you the power, the capacity and wealth of talent with which to venture out into the world and shine brightly, just like the sun overpowers darkness. So, I decided to 'step up and stand out' of the crowd. Because, it is my belief that in each and every one of us, there is a doctor, a lawyer, an engineer, a musician, a business mogul, the next Bill Gates or something greater, waiting to explode into a household name. Thus, I could not resist the urge to let the world hear of me and my gifts, despite the enemy within trying hard to convince me that I am not worth it. Who says that you have to belong in a box, where others possess the temerity to take the front seat and outshine you.

If, like me, you believe that there is an Almighty Creator, Jehovah, in heaven, who orchestrates all things good and all things bright and beautiful in the entire universe, then you would comprehend and share in my joy. Whilst writing this book, my true purpose became clear: it is to speak in order to transform people's lives without forgetting my Maker. He who knew my name, even before He formed me in my mother's womb and set me apart. (Jeremiah 1:4,5, NKJV). No, He did not just set me apart for no reason, but for greatness. He said that Dickson Aleroh, I know the plans I have for you, and they are to prosper you and not to harm you, plans to give you hope and a future. (Jeremiah 29:11, NKJV). As you can see, I am joyful to know that He has a purpose for me, and for you as well. Oh, what a great day it is, my friend.

When I think of this book, I see lives being transformed from mediocrity and perpetual failure, to one of purposeful living, overcoming insecurities, breakthroughs in all areas of life, the reclamation of lost identities, unveiling talents and winning ways. You are more than what the world has led you to believe, and within this book is a refreshing wealth of enlightenment and knowledge from an original mind. It was indeed inspired by God Almighty and I am not ashamed to state it, because deep down in my heart, I believe it to be so. Unlike most people in denial, I have seen both sides of the coin (that is, good and evil) and I know which side I would rather be and I promulgate it with confidence.

My experiences in life propelled me, my love for people's progress fuelled it and God Almighty, through some of my special friends, confirmed it; that this book has to impact this generation and many more to come. So, walk tall, because, no limitation nor insecurities can hinder your progress. Remember that you are made of heavenly steel which the enemy's words cannot penetrate.

Today's youths are compelled to seek comfort in gangs who often abuse illicit substances that will only exacerbate their situations. If only they would realise that the life they have been accustomed to is not that which has been purposed for them. To compound this further, the culture of fame and get rich quick schemes, which is widely promoted and glamorised on various television programmes, has rendered this generation lazy and overly complacent in their crooked ways. Unbeknown to them, that success comes at a price and must be paid without any shortcuts, as there are none in this regard.

In other cases, many have lost hope and walk around with chinks in their amour of confidence and wounded self-belief. Consequently, they lose their sense of worth. I know that life is too difficult as it is, but sometimes we are engulfed and distracted by all manner of issues. If you find yourself in such, do not fret, because, there is always a solution. After all, there's a light at the end of the tunnel, so, the difficulty you find yourself is not permanent. However, it won't change if you do not possess the will to want to turn things around for yourself. Beloved, this is your year to step up and stand out and not even your deepest fears can stop you.

Without further ado, I present to you this life-changing, thought-provoking and inspirational book that will challenge you to want to change your life for a better future. No matter what stage you are in life today, it will definitely prey deeply into your heart and rejuvenate the will-power, and activate the champion inside of you. Moreover, if indeed you believe that your destiny is in your hands, why waste it on fruitless endeavours? What have you got to lose by doing the contrary? It is time to step up to greatness, take control of your destiny and stand out of the pack. This is by far one of the potent routes you can adopt in order to attain your desired position in life. Your destiny is like a car, to unlock and make it move, there is need for a key, and the latter has been given to you by your Creator. If you don't use it, you will inevitably lose it, and continue to wallow in self-pity. Now, how do you achieve your dreams, identify your purpose in life, and lead an accomplished lifestyle? This book teaches just that and will open your mind to a world that says and understands, that we are capable and made of more than we have been led to believe. May God Almighty aid you in your journey and quest to enhance your status in life, as you peruse it.

# 1

# My Story, Testimony,
# And Journey To Success

*"Our deepest fear is not that we are inadequate. Our deepest fear is that we are powerful beyond measure. It is our light, not our darkness that most frightens us. We ask ourselves, who am I to be brilliant, gorgeous, talented, fabulous? Actually, who are you not to be? You are a child of God. Your playing small does not serve the world. There is nothing enlightened about shrinking so that other people won't feel insecure around you. We are all meant to shine, as children do. We were born to make manifest the glory of God that is within us. It's not just in some of us; it's in everyone. And as we let our own light shine, we unconsciously give other people permission to do the same. As we are liberated from our own fear, our presence automatically liberates others."*

*Marianne Williamson*

In life, as we go about our daily chores, time seems to slowly drift away like the night breeze. Indeed, there are three hundred and sixty five days in a typical year, and during these times, we engage ourselves in all manner of activities. While some are deeply, and intently immersed in thoughts, others simply wallow in idleness, and indulge themselves in things which bear little or no fruits in their lives. Suddenly, daylight slowly fade way, as if it were the pages of a captivating novel, being unravelled one leaf at a time.

Yet, we know not what secrets lurk in the subsequent pages. Nonetheless, we watch the sun rise in the morning, and set in the evening, without any care in the world to want to account for our achievements, and the conviction to assess the level of our individual productivity. What more, I wonder? But my anxiety further fuels my curiosity, as a child is filled with inquisitiveness. Not knowing, that, that which the eyes visualise, its meaning may not be what it seems nor should be. Perhaps, if he or she is patient enough, it may all become clearer in the end. As we cannot see the rear side of our bodies, so is the mystery of life. Our anxiety is further exacerbated by our curiosity to want to venture into the unknown, and with too many unknowns or blank pages, lies many questions. This for me is where life becomes all the more exciting.

If you have ever wondered where life could or would eventually take you, believe me, you are not alone. Surely, life is indeed a journey full of choices, trials and discoveries to be made. Nobody came into this world with any expectation, but with a mind full of it, because the world itself expects something of you. Though, since we arrived empty handed, in this same manner, shall we return.

In the late 1980s, growing up as a child in the then third world country, but, equally beautiful country of Nigeria, which is situated in the western part of the picturesque continent of Africa, life was not so easy. Sadly, today, in the 21st century, many children are still living and suffering in many parts of my continent and other parts of the world. Despite not having certain luxuries, such as, uninterrupted power supply, games consoles, sophisticated toys and the likes, as an average child would enjoy in the western world, we had to carry on with life. Sooner or later, it all became the norm and life simply continued, as if it was meant to be just the way it was.

At such an innocent age, the only worry in mind was to have a filling and befitting meal in my stomach. Sleeping, playing in the sand dunes, swimming in the local river, attending village events, listening to storytelling delivered by an elder, and engaging in all kinds of adventurous activities, became the order of the day for both myself and my brother. It was almost as if life was without any worries. But, little did we know that we were in for a shock.

If only kids were schooled on the pitfalls that life may throw at them later in life, so they would be better prepared to shoulder the storm when it came to shore.

Of course, I was never born into such a sorry situation as described above. My parents were well-to-do and at the early stages of my life as a child, I would not consider myself as lacking the best things in life. Although we were not the richest family on planet earth, my father always ensured that we did not have to go another day empty-bellied. He worked hard and I could recall during Christmas celebrations, my brother and I, were often bought our individual chicken. Happy days, right? Moreover, my mother was like my heaven, beautiful, resourceful, compassionate, loving and possessing a one-in-a-million smile.

Despite, these happy memories, little did I know that things were about to take a fascinating turn, one which would greatly impact me and my brother for the rest of our lives.

Sometimes, I wonder if war could have divided us as a family. That, I think, would have been somewhat comprehensible. Instead, calamity came knocking on our door and, from that moment onwards, my life as a child took a turn for the worse. First, the once flourishing marriage of my father and mother suddenly broke down. Consequently, my mother was forced to move out of the house, leaving myself and my younger brother with our father. Initially, it did not immediately dawn on us that our once loving home no longer existed. As time progressed, it became all the more apparent. Occasionally, I pondered on the whereabouts of my mother, and cried incessantly, due the void that I felt deep in my heart.

As if that wasn't bad enough, my father suddenly fell sick and was no longer able to perform his duties to us, due to his deteriorating health. For a few years we struggled, in hope that he would recover from the unknown illness and ordeal that he was experiencing. That was not to be, in fact, things got so severe that we had to drop out of school because our fees could not be afforded and, as a result, we were forced to concentrate on helping our father to hopefully get well again.

However, as his illness progressed and worsened, he had no

7

choice but to hand us over to his sister in the city. Here we were subjected to slavery, without due regards for our human rights and freedom. What really baffled us was that we were being treated as if she had a personal vendetta against my sick father.

On a particular occasion, I could remember vividly, being sent unsupervised with my brother, with plastic crates containing empty Coca-Cola glass bottles on our heads, to purchase some replenishments for the day. We had to walk over bridges on the highway and heaven help us if a single one should break. It would be met with the severest of punishments.

As you can imagine, at this stage, my confidence was at an all time low. It got so bad that we were not allowed to air our views and opinions and made to eat spoilt foods. Fear was instilled in us by way of unrelenting physical floggings and verbal abuse. It was like hell in an already disproportionate and wholly unfair world. Simply put, our worlds came crashing down right before our eyes. Seeing the debilitating situation we were being subjected to, onlookers would ask whose children we were.

Considering the sadness of our situation, we were taken to my paternal grandmother's village in Delta State, Nigeria, who, despite her best efforts, failed to bring any meaning to our already discombobulated lives. Unfortunately, we were made to serve drinks, in her local beer parlour, as I watched other kids going to school whilst we stayed at home in servitude. As you can imagine, with the trauma that I and my brother were experiencing, we completely lost all concentration and the last thing on our minds was to study. At that moment in time, the well-being of our father was most important to us. It was hoped that if he was able to regain his strength, life could return to normal for us.

Unbeknown to us, that was all wishful thinking. Whilst my father was battling to recover from both his deteriorating health and inability to attain mobility, we struggled to eat two square meals in any given day. At one point, we began improvising by manufacturing shoe polish from charcoal and candle wax to sell to passers-by. In the evenings, we would walk long distances to all corners of the village to pick up recyclable plastic containers from heaps of dirt so that we could afford our next meal of the day. Although, we were eventually allowed to go to school, the severity of our circumstances severely affected our ability to focus and assimilate all that was being taught. This led to my failure.

In order to quench our insatiable hunger for food, in the evenings, we [my brother and I], would go to the local ritual worshippers' shrine to eat their leftovers. Then in the morning, we would walk to the local river in our pants to catch some fish to cook. If fortune was on our side, we would make a reasonable catch. However, most times we would go hungry. This was the order of life for us as children.

However, I must credit my mother for trying to take us away from my father's relatives. But it was all beyond her power and control as they were hell-bent on keeping us. So the best she could do at the time was to send us some clothing during Christmas. Then, in 1994, the inevitable happened. Sadly, my father became deceased. Believe me, I could not cry because I had lost every will to even live, not to say of crying. I felt like I had lost both my identity and a part of my soul. Because, I loved my father so much, he was my everything and losing him was the greatest pain that I have ever felt. On that day, it was if my heart was ripped out of me and darkness suddenly clouded my world. The man who I looked up to was no longer alive. Sometimes, the void became too much to bear that I would cry in remembrance of the past memories of what I shared with him and what could have been.

From there onward, my life changed forever, and, as a consequence, I accepted my faith, grew quicker into a man and learnt to improvise along the way. If only my emotions would permit me to further expound on my not so pleasant experiences.

However, as they say, "*just when you think that it is over, that's when God takes over.*" Due to the relentless efforts and unwavering determination of my mother to get us out of the situation we found ourselves, a pastor was sent to pick us up and returned to my uncle in the city. Thereafter, I returned to school where I became a student of distinction. I was then made the class governor and then the head boy in the penultimate year of my secondary education in Lagos,

Nigeria.

Regardless of the demeaning nature of all I had endured with my brother, my drive to attain the best in life was never in question. As a matter of fact, my experiences served as the impetus to me strive for more out of life. Until then, I felt caged, anxious, lost, isolated and lacked confidence.

In fact, I saw education as the best way forward and dedicated most of my time studying and learning. It is my belief that knowledge is power and, if you have it, you can overcome the world, associate with men and women of high repute, hold intelligent conversations, walk confidently, influence people and command respect among your peers.

These values were imprinted in me by my uncle who sadly passed away a few years ago. In him I found a hero and a man who epitomised the qualities to emulate. This man completely changed my life for the better and my way of thinking was totally transformed. Finally, I was out of the hooks and could now concentrate on my journey to regaining my lost identity and years of indescribable pain and despair.

My late uncle taught me all I know about education, uprightness and integrity. He was truly a breath of fresh air in my life. To boost my confidence, during the early morning Sunday service at church, he often encouraged me to deliver presentations in front of the congregation. Although I use to stutter badly, due to my experiences, I realised that it was an uphill battle that I had to fight and overcome in earnest.

Now in my adult years, I battled through speech difficulties and fears. From presentation to presentation, I would struggle harder and harder. Sometimes it was shameful and imperfect, but I persevered. Thanks to God Almighty, I am able to speak in public with great confidence, despite all. It shows that if you believe in Him, you will become unstoppable and victorious in all battles.

They say, "*a quitter never wins and a winner never quits.*" Thus, in many areas of my life, I often go the extra mile to be the best and, I never let my hang-ups limit me in any way. People who know me would attest to the fact that I am not a quitter and always fighting to the end regardless of the difficulties that I am presented with.

Today, I am the first in my family that can boast of three degrees, including two masters and a doctorate in Chemistry from top class UK institutions (Imperial College London, Queen Mary University of London, and Southampton University). In 2007 I was awarded, together, with my first masters degree, the Royal Society of Chemistry Downland prize for the best Chemistry project.

Over the years, I have embraced entrepreneurship to set up businesses in the solar energy, consumer electronics, coaching, public speaking and mentoring. In addition, I have been privileged to be employed in the chemical industry. In a million years, if anyone had told me that I will be elevated to such a height and beyond, I would have very much doubted it. But God Almighty has a purpose for all and, despite the obstacles that may be in your way, you will surely overcome if you remain steadfast and pray with your eyes firmly set on Him.

When God Almighty has purposed you for a specific task, He would bring you out of the rubble to make you into that exceptional person He designed you to be. This is my testimony to the goodness and faithfulness of our Creator, God Almighty, in my life. He deemed me worthy of such magnanimous favour, and made me the envy of many and a cornerstone to my family.

This is the essence of this book and the reason why I will remain forever indebted to Him. Beloved, it is my belief that anything is possible if you strive hard enough and persevere with prayers. Remember, it worked for me and so it can also transform your life for the better. God Almighty has always been the centre-point of my life, irrespective of my imperfections. He is real and I can testify of his magnificent works. I hope my story has inspired you and will continue to do so. And believe me, you can be anything you want to be if you put your mind to it.

# 2

# The Stifling Power Of Fear

*"The first duty of a man is to conquer fear; he must get rid of it, he cannot act till then."*

*Thomas Carlyle*

The term fear is a state of mind and is undeniably the most prevalent emotion that all humans share, right from the inception of creation until now and this isn't about to change anytime soon. Frankly speaking, to many individuals the mere mention of fear itself is enough to create a multitude of fears in their minds. Therefore, it is not surprising that the former President of the United State of America, Franklin Roosevelt, once famously orated that, *"the only thing we have to fear is fear itself."* That said, the nature of our individual or collective fears and our relative susceptibilities to them, differs greatly.

Moreover, this does not take away from the fact that the majority of fears we experience are innate and deeply ingrained within us due to situations that are sometimes beyond our control. Most people seem to believe or want to believe that fear is wholly physical and completely ignore the spiritual aspect which I think is most important. So follow me as I delve into the world of fear and prescribe ways of navigating your way out of it.

*Q. Take a Moment's Pause and Ask Yourself These Questions.*

Have you ever wondered why some peculiar individuals appear more comfortable when presented with situations, involving public speaking, high-speed car racing, surfing, skydiving and others of similar precarious nature? Have you felt apprehensive simply by the thought of embarking on a new venture, moving homes, starting a new relationship, relocating to an unfamiliar location or, perhaps, during interviews? Have you experienced a surge in adrenaline or increased activity in your brain prior to delivering an impromptu or even a previously planned presentation to a group of individuals in a social gathering or colleagues at your place of work? Is being unsure about what the future holds and the notion of failure raised the hair at the back of your head? If your answers to these questions are yes, then you are certainly not in the minority.

## The Many Faces and Types of Physical Fear

The truth is that the aforementioned questions are very valid, but they only create what I refer to as "physical fear." This is the type of fear which is apparent and visible on the outward appearance and has its origins in our inward misconceptions. A young man I once encountered shared with me an event that occurred at a burial ceremony he attended. On this particular occasion, he was assigned the task of delivering a brief eulogy about the deceased. Immediately, he became frightened due to the upsurge of negative thoughts in his mind and consequently he declined to take on the task on the grounds of a feverish condition.

Not surprising, as the conversation progressed, he stated that "he would rather be found resting in the coffin, than to be the one tasked with presenting the eulogy of the deceased." I am sure that most of us would understand why this seemingly confident, at first glance, looking man may have abstained in the first instance. This is the power of fear in action and for many individuals, when a duty such as to do with speaking in front of an audience is presented to them in advance, a stream of negative thoughts begin to cloud their thoughts. As a consequence, most immediately cave in and think of excuses not to go forth with the impending task.

Fear is so powerful that, it cripples all thoughts, deprives logical reasoning and stifles positive progression if not dealt with outright. Perhaps the most interesting evidence of this was highlighted by a female student I met at a public speaking class. Initially, in order to break the ice, I started by asking why she was at the gathering. Her reply was somewhat unexpected. She stated that whenever she is about to give a speech in a public setting, she simply 'fainted' and is fed up of being taken to the hospital for treatment each time she makes a presentation.

Understandably, this came to me as a complete shock having not previously heard of such adverse reaction to this peculiar fear of speaking in public. The truth of the matter is that most people harbouring such extreme reaction to fear are mostly very confident and humorous on the outward appearance. They are often very skilful at masking their inward insecurities and propensity to fear.

Paradoxically, most people may never remember their experience during birth, but may recall their reactions to the first time, as a baby, that they were tossed into the air, heard a loud bang or a knock, or were left alone in a room. Indeed, it is a universally agreed fact that all humans were born with three innate physical fears. These include the fear of height (Acrophobia), noise (Phonophobia), and of neglect (separation anxiety). Moreover, these fears are only cautionary and make us more conscious of the common dangers around us.

It is a popular misconception that fear is the same a phobia. Of course, this is far from the truth. By definition, fear can be described as an apprehensive sensation which breeds the belief that something or a situation is noxious or represents a danger. Whilst phobia is simply an irrational fear of anything or an imaginative situation. In recent years, psychologists have come up with 5 subsections (ego-death, extinction, loss of autonomy, mutilation and separation) out of which all other "supposed" physical fears are based.

*Ego-death*: This encompasses the fear of being shamed, humiliated, loss of integrity, self-disapproval and the disintegration of our constructed sense of self-worth and capabilities. Under this category, public speaking, social exclusion and reclusiveness (self-withdraw) are common examples.

*Obliteration*: The fear of ceasing to exist or annihilation comes under this section. In addition, the phobia of height, insects and the likes are included here.

*Loss of Self-determination*: This covers the loss of independence, immobility, entrapment or inability to control one's circumstances, particularly, to do with relationships and illness.

*Accident*: This pertains the fear of the loss of precious body parts. An individual with such fear, dreads being attacked by animals, insects or another someone bearing a sharp object.

*Isolation*: Last, but not least, this relates to the fear of being separated from loved ones, rejection, abandonment or isolation.

For many years, numerous practising psychologists in various institutions around the world have attempted to narrow down the source of physical fear and to provide a logical explanation as to why its dysphoric effects vary from person to person. Moreover, most of the evidence to date is merely speculative.

In my candid opinion, fear may arise from a combination of factors instead of just a single source. For instance, an individual can develop fear by being involved in or witnessing a motor accident, experiencing a traumatic attack in an isolated and dark alleyway, or any other event that directly threatens his or her chances of survival. In fact, the list of causes may be endless and since fear is part of the human fabric, all that can be done to alleviate it is to muster the confidence to control and, eventually, dominate it (*vide infra*).

According to research carried out by Edward Binder at the California State University, Northridge, USA, there is irrefutable evidence that alludes to the fact that most physical fears are borne out of the environment in which we were nurtured and grew up, which I can relate to.

## Spiritual Fear: Fighting the Inner Demons

As far as I am aware, most mainstream motivational and inspirational books which attempt to tackle this aspect of personal development (that is, the subject of fear), often shy away from delving into this crucial aspect of spiritual fear. One probable reason may be that they are misled by the notion that the people of the 21st century or so called, 'computer age,' do not want to be made aware of anything that will undermine their view of such personal issue(s) from an objective standpoint. So they try their possible best to steer away from this not so obvious, but most imperative type of fear, which has its origin in the supernatural domain. Despite their arrant oblivity and ignorance, there is undisputed evidence that spiritual fear exists and must be approached with a high degree of seriousness.

Irrespective of your stance on this issue, I implore you to read on. For instance, in horror movies, such as the Omen, SAW, Exorcist, Dracula, Unborn and the like, there is a clear depiction of evil and repulsive scenes that are designed to create a specific kind of fear within the target audience. Some people, (especially, kids) who watch such movies, often say that, when asleep, their dreams are often clouded with all sort of dangerous situations and some see beings which they say bear semblance to those in the horror movies. This invariably creates a mental picture of fear to the extent that some suddenly wake up in the middle of the night and begin to panic.

Have you ever wondered why they are afraid and what created this fear in the first instance? This is simply because the unseen remains a mystery to many today and, together with their lack of a comprehensive understanding of the vices of the unknown, further intensifies their fear of its capabilities. For some, the mere mention of spirits automatically generates a sensation of fear in their minds and this makes it more important that we are aware of this issue of spiritual fear and how it affects our life progression.

Spiritual fear is the most powerful tool used by the enemy to manipulate, control, enslave and prevent its subjects from accomplishing their God-given destiny. One must be mindful or otherwise you can be destroyed by it. Thankfully, you should be reassured by the fact that, our Creator (God Almighty) is not the author of spiritual fear. However, He created us with the opposite and that is with good intentions, without any restrictions on our liberty, happiness, level of fulfilment and level of attainment. In fact, on the issue of spiritual fear, the holy scriptures stated that, *"For God has not given us the spirit of fear (timid or cowardice), but of power, of love and of a sound mind (self-control and self-discipline)."* (2 Timothy 1:7, NKJV) Furthermore, in the book of Romans 8: 15 (NKJV), we are led to understand that, *"we did not receive the spirit that makes us a slave unto fear, but a spirit of sonship."* As you can see, it is an undisputable fact that God wants his children to be happy, but the enemy also has his own agenda and that is to inflict us with fear so as to preclude us from our true purpose.

A typical example of such preclusion in action is in the area of career. I was quite perplexed to discover that, after graduating from high school or University, a huge chunk of graduates do not end up working in their field of study. Most end up settling for menial jobs and others later discover that their passions are not in line with the field in which they spent the good part of three to four years of their lives. In other cases, these graduates are too afraid to apply for higher postgraduate degree such as PhDs, because they are too afraid of being rejected and most begin to question their intelligence. These are the enemy's vices or spiritual fear in action. It breeds doubt, lack of self-confidence and self-deprivation.

Of course, spiritual fear can be conquered through the awesome power of Jehovah (God Almighty) and his intervention. So why fear at all. After all, God says (through His prophet Isaiah), *"Do not be afraid, you will not suffer shame. Do not fear disgrace, you will not be humiliated. You will forget the shame of your youth and remember no more the reproach of your widowhood."* (Isaiah 54: 4, NIV)

## Fear: My Personal Experience

We all have experiences of fear (both physical and spiritual) of some sort, with similarities and disparities. In my case, I could recall as a child growing up in the absence of a father and mother, I had to endure maltreatment at the hands of my extended family members (that is, uncles and aunts). The very people I thought I could trust. However, my hopes were dashed and sometimes the punishments I endured were so severe, that I wondered if there was a God at all.

As I approached adulthood, the psychological effects evolved and materialised into low confidence, lack of self-expressiveness and poor social interaction skills, to name a few. So I want you to understand that the environment of upbringing matters a great deal to children. Now, as a father of two, my experiences have allowed me to cherish the time I spend with my kids and, with each passing day, I strive to do my best by them. Discouragement kills a child's confidence and should not be encouraged or tolerated in any society.

On another occasion, at the tender age of about 5 years old, an incident occurred which made me realise that I was afraid of heights. One day, my late father took me and my brother up a footbridge which ran across a busy highway. As we progressed toward the centre of the bridge, I became overwhelmed by fear and began to lose my composure. Suddenly, I heard my father yelling, by way of "persuasion and encouragement", that I should walk towards him. By doing this, the fears were softened and I was able to walk with some courage.

That was the motivation I needed at that point in time and it surely helped a great deal, as I was able to meet and hold his hand as we descended down the other side of the bridge. Although, until this present day I am still fighting to overcome this fear of heights, the encouragement from my father meant a lot to me and boosted my confidence. This is what we all need in our lives, to help break free from the shackles of physical fear.

Do you have someone positive in your life who encourages you?

If not, you need to find yourself a friend, a partner or a mentor who can provide you with encouragement and support. Many teenagers are lost to gangs on the street of London (UK) and elsewhere in the world due in part to the lack of encouragement from a well meaning adult and poor self-confidence.

Whilst in Africa, during my early teenage years, I had already built up a reputation as a straight "A" student and as result, at the age of 14, I was already in the final year of my secondary education and was given the position of the acting head boy of my school. Despite this early achievement, I was still haunted by one more fear. This was public speaking (glossophobia). As a final year undergrad, I was told to give a presentation on my master degree project, but was too petrified to do so. It was almost as if I was about to be attacked by a pack of dogs. However, after I had given my speech, a lady lecturer called out my name and gave me the thumbs up. "Well done!" she said.

Once again, I was encouraged by that simple gesture from her. Notwithstanding this drawback, at that time I remained resolute and undeterred by my determination to succeed to the highest possible level. Therefore, instead of simply throwing in the towel and conceding defeat, I forged ahead, rolled up my sleeves and worked even harder to get to the highest possible level in my chosen career. Today, here I am, a fully qualified and practising PhD chemistry specialist, a brewing entrepreneur, life coach, and a transformational speaker. You too can do the same today, if only you are willing to put in your best efforts.

Dear friend, I am evidence that hard work and persistence pays off in the end. Today, in many relationships, women are defamed by way of physical abuse and are often too afraid and reluctant to leave their abusive partners, all under the guise of family cohesion or loss of comfort. A relationship, like any other, is supposed to be enjoyed, not endured. I know of a young woman, living in the United Kingdom, who was married to a man who was 15 years older. Despite bearing him four children, the abuse she suffered only worsened. In other situations, he would scold her in front of his friends so to appear as if he was a man in total control of his household.

This lasted for many years, until she finally conjured up the courage and gave him a final ultimatum to either stop the violence or risk the devolution of their marriage. As it happened, he chose to continue in his abusive ways. Eventually, when she couldn't take it any longer, she picked up the phone and called the police who came to her rescue. She then instituted divorce proceedings. Although no one prays for a marriage breakup, this wasn't a situation that she could sustain further. In this case, she had the courage to say no, enough is enough! You too can do the same today and say no to fear.

At your place of work, you may be the victim of rampant bullying and discrimination by your superiors or jealous colleagues. Consequently, it causes you to question your self-worth and competence. Be not afraid to stand up for yourself and don't let the fear of the inevitable eventuality deprive you of victory. For those individuals who are vying to own their own businesses, don't shy away from taking risks. Like the popular saying goes, *"there is no gain without pain."* The same applies to success. Without risk it cannot be attained and nothing can be achieved.

Fear is the number one enemy of progression, self-fulfilment and prominence. Therefore, whatever your dreams and aspirations are, go for it and don't allow fear to deter you.

## Overcoming the Power of Fear

It is indeed true that fear is an obstacle to unlocking and harnessing our innermost and absolute potential. In the majority of cases, most people seem to lack and are often unwilling to obtain those skills that are vital to mastering the art of overcoming the suppressive power of fear in their lives.

That is not to say that some fears are not rational and must be tackled with some degree of caution. It may appear surprising to some at the revelation that some key fears were deliberately ingrained within us from birth, so as to make us more aware, and conscious of the dangers around us. However, as we approach adulthood, some fears (in the form of phobias) begin to surface due to misconceptions gained from external environmental influences. Suddenly, we are presented with a predicament on how best to approach the fears we experience and have become accustomed to. As the great and knowledgeable, Dr Martin Luther King Jr., famously orated, that:

*"Normal fear protects us, abnormal fear motivates us to want to improve our individual and collective welfare, abnormal fear poisons and distorts our inner lives. Our problem is not to be rid of fear, but to harness and master it."*

The aforementioned quote seems to provide the tools to aid us in tackling our fears. Furthermore, I am pretty sure that by applying some due diligence, we can extract some sense from it. Therefore, in order to overcome one's fear, it requires a simple principle and that is to learn to "harness and master" them If you do this, you will begin to see some noticeable and positive changes in different areas of your life, especially in areas such as engagements, impromptu speeches and speaking in a large gathering.

Here are 7 proposed key nuggets to add to your armoury in your quest to harness, master and overcome your fears.

*Audacity*

This is perhaps the most important prerequisite of all. Why put in so much hard work, only to aim low and achieve poorly? The greater the success you desire, the bolder you need to be. Low thinkers accomplish less in life, while bold thinkers have no limits. So, think big, take big steps and achieve big things. Many people would agree that to be able to achieve any feat in life, one has to possess an unflinching audacity. Multi-billionaires and tycoons of the present day started small, but had "bigger" visions. As a result, electronics giants, such as, the likes of Microsoft, Apple, Panasonic, Samsung and others, were able to build up billions of dollars of revenue and a presence all over the world over a period of time. This is evidence that, in the absence of audacity, most will never be able to stand up to their deep-seated fears and begin to climb to prominence.

## *Selfless determination*

In any area of your life, to attain greater heights you have to want it. How strongly you want something will be evident in your selfless determination and drive.

So take a moment and ask yourself these set of questions. Is fear holding me back from landing that dream job, that promotion, embarking on a new direction in my career endeavours career or from implementing that 'big' idea you've had in mind for many years now? Do I possess the determination to change my current status? Your answer to these questions will help to activate your selfless determination. Moreover, do you remember how you felt, the first time you decided to embark on a quest to obtained a professional drivers licence? Surely, you were excited and resolute in your determination to finally master the art of driving, and the prospect of becoming a professional.

This same analogy applies when trying to overcome fear. For self-determination fuels one's burning desires, and in turn, enhances our probability of accomplishing lasting success. Ultimately, fear becomes a thing of the past.

## *Self-motivation*

The motivation to achieve a particular goal in life is a paramount catalyst to possess and is needed to make that first move and, crucially, to keep the ball rolling. For a car to successfully move from one point to another, the first action of the driver is to initiate the ignition, apply the correct gear and then accelerate. The acceleration in this case serves to motivate the car to attain mobility and bring you to your intended destination. In essence, it is pertinent to always motivate yourself, and when it seems that things are not going according to plan, put it all away, take a breather and return with a rejuvenated mindset.

I have experienced this first hand during my doctoral training. In many instances an experiment goes awry and you are suddenly overwhelmed by a feeling of disappointment and, to compound it all, you have a deadline to meet. At this point, panic and fear sets in. But, when you are motivated, you feel uplifted and begin to rationalise about the areas of failure you encountered, and why they occurred at all. Then, a resolution becomes apparent and fear is no longer in your mind. This is one secret that most people who find themselves in certain difficult situations don't understand. Instead, they struggle to overcome their fears because they do not possess the motivation to seek a remedy.

*Courage*

This is an important attribute to have in your quest to overcome any insecurities (including, fear) you may have. Today, people with known difficulties often aren't willing to confront them head-on, because they simply cannot garner enough courage to do so. Martin Luther King Jr stated that, *"We must build dikes of courage to hold back the flood of fear."* So what are you waiting for? Stand up and make a move. Be of good courage.

*Consistent Practise*

As the saying goes, *"practise makes perfect."* Nonetheless, contrary to what you may have read in other inspirational books, practising is not enough to help you overcome your fear. Consistency is key and when you combine it with your practising regime, then you have a winning formula. A note of advice, when you have identified your fear, you have to constantly engage it. This is done through practise and doing it consistently in those situations where you feel most uncomfortable.

For instance, if your fear has to do with public speaking, enrol yourself into a speaking group or society where they have regular meetings. In addition, during the meetings, you should always volunteer to present and partake in impromptu speeches. In no distant future, you will become a master to your fears, and no longer be enslaved by them. So, in order to master your fears, you need to adopt the culture of constant practise, whenever and wherever the opportunity arises. The bottom line is that, no one can master anything without persistent practising.

### Self-belief

This is a powerful attribute to have, if you don't already have it. If you do not believe in yourself, no one else will. In order to climb a mountain, a climber has to first believe that he or she has the capability to surmount it. Moreover, this is also applicable to the area of fear. The latter sows negative beliefs within us in order to deny us the opportunity to attempt certain things in life. Begin to believe and trust in your capacity to overcome your worst fears, and it will come to fruition.

### Support

I cannot stress this enough, it is imperative to foster a sustainable support network or environment, while trying to overcome your deepest and most worrisome fears. We all need someone to encourage us and this could be a friend, a family member, and the like. Remember, a supportive environment provides a fertile ground for positivity and success to flourish.

Although, there are other recommendations published in many literatures out there for overcoming all manner of fears, you should always remember that the secret to achieving this is within you. But it is our individual responsibility to harness our inner powers in this regard. So, what's holding you back? You owe it to yourself to defeat fear and you can.

# 3

# Finding True Purpose and Fulfilment

*"Life finds its purpose and fulfilment, in the expansion of happiness."*

*Maharishi Mahesh Yogi*

In life, as we transit from one situation to another, we often find ourselves in the dark as to what our God-given purpose in life is and how we can become fulfilled and contented in our lives. This causes us to begin to assess our status and the direction in which we are tending to, be it in our careers or day-to-day lives. Consequently, we begin to subconsciously harbour some quite valid questions in our minds and often don't know from where or whom to seek the right answers.

As a naive teenager, although I was quite focused in school, my purpose was not immediately apparent. Therefore, very early in life I began to ask myself the following questions; Why am I here? How did I come to be? What is the purpose of my existence? Where does my fulfilment lie? What is the right religion to follow? Am I on the right path in my life and, if not, who would direct me accordingly, seeing that I had no father figure to run to? Who is my creator? Why did He allow certain incidents to occur in my life? As an adult, I have come to understand the reasons for these questions, as the answers are now becoming more apparent as I grew older.

Take, for instance, the human body. Isn't it amazing that every part has a specific function to perform and no two dissimilar parts can perform the same functions? Yet they all work cohesively to achieve a collective goal which is to keep the body functioning on a daily basis, and make our lives easier to manage. Such is the uniqueness of humans. Interestingly, we are all here to perform a specific task in this complex universe we find ourselves. This is our purpose. A purpose is the reason for which something or someone exist, and one which must be fulfilled.

Despite the validity of our questions, there is one ultimate question of all and that is, where and how to go about finding the 'right' answers. Could it be from more experienced relatives, friends, counsellors, fortune tellers, psychics or a higher power? The truth is that, in the majority of cases, most well-meaning individuals, in their desperation, often go to the wrong sources for answers. Not knowing that what they need is diligence and patience in their quest for solution and direction.

## Seeking Answers to Your Purpose

The bottom line is that to every problem there is always an unequivocal solution. There are two things that all humans seek in life and these, to some extent, determine our happiness and longevity here on earth. They are, (i) the affirmation of our individual purpose and (ii) the likelihood of the latter to bring about fulfilment, happiness, success and contentment.

The good news is that there is one credible source (our Creator) from which we can find the answers to our purpose and a lasting fulfilment. The source that I am referring to is superior to any other and it is 'God Almighty' (if you are a believer). Beloved, no psychologist, coach, motivator or counsellor which rely solely on their earthly knowledge can help you find true answers as to where your purpose on earth lies. This is why the Holy Scriptures (NKJV) affirmed that, *"my people are destroyed for lack (or inexistence) of knowledge."* (Hosea 4:6)

You see, in times of difficulties and crisis, we tend to wallow in self-pity, depressive thoughts, the questioning of one's self-worth, adhering to negative criticism and even go as far as contemplating suicide. Not knowing that God uses such events to test us, build our character and prepare us for the successes to come. Thus, I urge you to never give up because it is during such times, when we can see no way out of our situation, that God steps in, to reveal to us our true purpose (after diligently seeking him) and elevates us to places we never envisaged. Unfortunately, most people still don't realise this, so they try all kinds of avenues and fail woefully, because they lack the knowledge of God's infinite power and purpose for their lives.

For instance, when a car develops a fault, where would you take it for repair? You won't take it to a hospital, but to a trained mechanic or, better still, the manufacturer. In other words, the creator or inventor has the blueprint and therefore knows the reasons why that item has been created. Similarly, our Creator is the only one who holds the answers to all our questions.

Now, what is this knowledge that the bible alluded to? It is simply the inexhaustible knowledge of the one and only living JEHOVAH (God Almighty). In the book of Romans 10:17 (NKJV), we are led us to understand that, "*So then faith comes by hearing and hearing by the word of God.*" The 'word' of God bears great power and what greater power is there on earth or beyond that can be compared to that of God Almighty himself? Simply none! Moreover, the word of God is life and holds the key to all our desires.

Dear friend, "*God is not a man that He should lie. Nor a Son of man, that He should repent. Has He said and will He not do? Or Has He spoken and will He not make it good?*" (Numbers 23:19, NKJV) You can be reassured that the purpose of God concerning your life will not and I reiterate, will never lapse without it being accomplished. To further confirm this, the bible states that, "*For assuredly, I say to you, till heaven and earth pass away, one jot or one tittle will by no means pass from the law (not one small letter or stroke shall pass, according to the new American standard bible), till all is fulfilled.*" (Matthew 5:18; 24:35; Luke 21:33, NKJV). This is clear evidence that God wants us to be fulfilled in this life and beyond only if you can seek him with faith and the reason for your creation will made clear unto you.

So quit worrying about that temporary situation in which you find yourself. Seek God diligently and march on. Never give up until you win. Remember that, *"you can do all things through Christ who strengthens you."* (Philippians 4:13, NKJV) Therefore, when people scold and mock you due to your current situation do not be weary, because now you have the understanding that God wants you to be fulfilled and that He has a set purpose for your life which will surely be accomplished, period.

The devil knows this truth and that is why those who God has chosen often experience great difficulties and adverse situations. However, God allows this because out of this comes forth the development of a well fortified character and the ascertaining of one's true purpose.

Stop relying on your human knowledge where solutions are greatly limited. Rather tap into the infinite fountain of spiritual knowledge of our Creator (God Almighty). For it is written that, *"the wisdom of this world is foolishness in God's sight. As it is written, "He catches the wise in their craftiness."* (1 Corinthians 3:19; Job 5:13, NKJV). Our earthly knowledge has limitations, but, heavenly knowledge is infinite and more potent than any other.

## How to Identify Your True Purpose

This is a question that we often ask ourselves as we get older and wiser. In the book of Genesis 1:28 (NKJV), it is written that, *"God blessed them and said to them, Be fruitful and increase in number; fill the earth and subdue it. Rule over the fish in the sea and the birds in the sky and over every living creature that moves on the ground."*

Beloved, I urge you to meditate on the above paragraph in times when you feel lost because this is the collective purpose of all humanity summarised in a single paragraph.

Therefore, if you want to find your true purpose, I challenge you to invest some time to search and harness the undiluted truth in God's word today and see if your life will not begin to transform for the better.

As you have seen, from the inception of creation, man's purpose on earth was already been laid down in clear detail, but, today many are still oblivious of this fact. In all areas of our lives we are suppose to increase (accretion, breakthrough, aggrandizement or accumulation), be fruitful (multiply, flourish, blossom, proliferate, successful or rich), fill the earth and subdue (dominate, overcome or conquer) and rule (be the predator and not the prey). There lies your God-given purpose and destiny, on a nutshell, and these are things that we can all enjoy to the fullest.

So, if you are struggling and not satisfied, then it is time to reconnect with your Godly purpose. This is the only way you can be fulfilled and successful in life. When you find your purpose and destiny, then you will be at peace with yourself.

In my case, upon attaining two master degree and a PhD at such a young age, I thought that I had found my true purpose, until I was told by a pastor to seek God's counsel concerning my life and that he reveals things in magnificent ways. Before now, I have always relied on my human knowledge, but I noticed no tangible results. So, I did as instructed and the results were astonishing. You too can do the same today, because God has designed you for a purpose that is beyond all human imagination. The reason you are still in the wrong place is because you haven't realigned yourself with your heavenly purpose.

Believe it or not, University education is not suitable for everybody. Your purpose may be in acting, singing, business, invention or a sport. But you have to first seek ways to pinpoint where your true purpose lies and remember that your purpose is different from that of James or John. So stop following other people's careers.

If you take a look at the list of the Times top ten university dropouts of all time, you will find people like; Bill Gates (entered Harvard University in 1973, only to drop out after 2 years to start Microsoft with his childhood friend, Paul Allen), Steve Jobs (Apple, Pixar and NeXT computer founder, dropped out of Reed College just after 6 months due to financial constraints), Frank Lloyd Wright (dropped out of University of Wisconsin-Madison

1887, now America's most celebrated Architect), Buckminster Fuller, James Cameron (the creator of star wars), Mark Zuckerberg (founder of Facebook), Tom Hanks, Harrison Ford and Tiger Woods. Why are they so successful and fulfilled today? It is simply because there was a renaissance and a re-alignment of purpose with that of God.

Though, it may take many years of trial and error, you will surely identify your true purpose. Remember that your purpose is tied to your success, and the latter to fulfilment.

## Keys to Unlock Your True Purpose

1. Engage your Creator (God Almighty), seek His counsel by studying the holy scriptures and apply the principles therein.
2. Create time to better understand yourself, away from all distractions.
3. Identify and nurture your passion, talents and leanings.
4. Find a place or an organisation where you can develop the tools that will help you identify and better harness those skills you never knew you had.
5. Trust your instincts and don't be afraid to try multiple ideas, until you find the one that gives you lasting satisfaction, happiness and contentment.
6. Embrace positive changes and evolve with time. Because, as you grow, you may decide that a certain career direction does not fit well with your leanings.
7. Listen to your heart, then set out and persist on the course that feels right to you.
8. Connect with people of like minds, so that your purpose can shine through.
9. Stay on a course, even if you do not possess the qualifications for it.
10. Learn from experiences as you go and never be too afraid of mistakes and failure.

11. Remain assured and do not be perturbed, it may surprise you that your purpose might just be in something that you least expect.

A prominent man of God (Sam Adeyemi) once stated that, *"if your purpose is in line with God's, then success is guaranteed."* In other words, when you find your purpose, then everything else will begin to fall into place. Moreover, I am absolutely convinced that in your God-given purpose lies your place of fulfilment, success and ultimately, lasting happiness. Therefore, I urge you to take these little steps of faith today and watch your Creator multiply them into mighty achievements in your life.

# 4

# Walking The Narrow Path To Success

*"Take up one idea. Make that one idea your life - think of it, dream of it, live on that idea. Let the brain, muscles, nerves, every part of your body, be full of that idea and just leave every other idea alone. This is the way to success."*

*Swami Vivekananda*

Success is the single most common asset that we all vie for today and yet many still don't fully comprehend the process, character fortitude, principles, virtues and challenges involved. Today, most people simply want success, but don't want to work for it. To the wise, I say, "think twice before you speak, because your words and influence will plant the seed of either success or failure in the mind of another." (Napoleon Hill) Bearing this in mind, I urge you to read this carefully, as these words may hopefully awaking your hearts and minds to begin to activate your innermost desires for a prosperous change in your life.

Success to many people can mean different things and is somewhat based on their ideologies, maturity, accomplishments and experiences. For instance, in this day and age, most teenagers view success as having a nice car, plush apartments, lots of money in the bank, being famous and being noticed by beautiful women. These may be considered by the older generation as being naive and immature by the more experienced ones amongst us.

However, I would hesitate a little from joining the bandwagon of those who are of the notion that simply because these teenagers have such wrong preconceptions of the meaning of success, then they must be detached from reality. Perhaps we ought to look more closely at the reason why they have such a belief in the first place.

After observing and speaking to many youths over the years, I am able to narrow down their perception of success to what is portrayed in the media. Gone are the days when kids were supposed to go to school, study hard and get a high paying job upon graduation. Nowadays the philosophy of success has been so adversely tainted by the display of easy and deceitful wealth in music (hip-hop, pop and rap) videos and the enticement of the calibre of near-perfect women you can attract that children now view the idea of hard work as being a thing of the past.

Most now believe that they can completely abandon innovative thinking, original creativity, inventiveness and improvisation for illicit activities, which would eventually lead to a brush with the law of the land and, ultimately, put them in jail. As the saying goes, "easy come, easy go." In other words, if one embraces the culture of hard work and remains steadfast, then he or she paves the way for long-lasting success.

I like to view success as a process which consists of periods of failures and challenges. The former being the most important and, depending on your approach, your journey could lead to either a successful end or outright futility. Be not deceived, if you are not prepared to accept failures and challenges, then you are not ready to succeed in life. Today, many people still don't realise that success and failure are intertwined and completely inseparable. "According to the Winston Churchill, "Success consists of going from failure to failure without the loss of enthusiasm."

This is what you have to bear in mind, that success doesn't come cheaply at all and it requires more than you think. However, don't despair. You will get there. It's only a matter of time and having the breadth of character to tackle whatever life throws at you.

## Understanding the Principles and Price of Success

Success to many people can be interpreted based on their individual understanding of the process it entails. Similarly, in our daily lives, we pick up new ideas as we progress, which is a testament to the complications of life itself. However, in the realm of success, I want you to be aware that there are a host of lessons to be learnt, but, the proceeding quotes highlights four pertinent ones out of many others.

It is undoubtedly true that, "you cannot eat your cake and have it." And, "you should not expect to harvest, if you do not first sow a single seed." Importantly, "the level of success you achieve today, weighs heavily on the measure of work and focus you invest in the goals you set in your daily life." Last, but not least, "you can only achieve and attain as high as you set the bar."

In this age of increased awareness, it beggars belief that at every turn there is no shortage of people with an insatiable appetite for magnanimous success, absolute happiness and fulfilment. Yet the majority are ingenuously oblivious of the principles and sacrifices involved in order to accomplish them. For every success and milestone you attain in life, there is a price to pay. Take for instance, a boxing contest, when two athletes steps into the ring, their target goal is to win the title and champions belt on offer.

Nevertheless, for the belt to be won, both athletes have to first engage in a fierce battle. Certainly, this would eventually lead to the two participants suffering serious bruises and, in the worst case scenario, both may end up being admitted to hospital for treatment. Although, the prize can be won ultimately by only one of the contestants, both the winner and loser pay the price for their quest for superiority in the boxing arena. Such is the price of success and, as in other spheres of life; we will all pay it in one way or another in our journey to our place of fulfilment and success.

Now, let's look at the principles of success. One such principle, that is sometimes ignored, pertains to the concept of 'sowing'. In other words, that which one plants or invests in order to get a return. Interestingly, this may not be monetary, but things such as time, strength (mental and physical), deprivation of sleep and pleasures, blood and sweat. Just like a farmer whose primary source of living is, for example, the sale of corn. At inception of the planting season, he prepares the soil on his land to ensure that it is indeed fertile and then sows some seeds.

For the next couple of months he tirelessly waters, maintains and monitors the development of his crops. From my personal experience, I can attest to the arduous labour, persistence and patience involved in the farming process. Failure to follow this said process could lead to disaster and, worse still, becoming poor due to having no yield(s) when others are harvesting their matured crops for sale. On the contrary, if it all goes well, he reaps handsomely and earns a lot of money for his survival and that of his immediate family. Therefore, don't expect any reward if you don't invest anything.

Crucially, while the imperativeness of sowing is stressed, the nature of investment you make could either lead to hugely profitable outcomes or downright forfeiture. Thus you need to do your homework properly and diligently to ensure that you are not simply walking blindly into a potentially futile venture.

Sincerely, no well-meaning individual attains success without applying some 'due diligence'. According to the Chinese philosopher Confucius, *"the expectations of life depend upon due diligence; a mechanic that would perfect his work, must first sharpen his tools."* To come by any good fortune, you need to be diligent in both the planning and execution stages. In other words, invest a great deal of time in the perusal and perfection of your act in order to avert perpetual failure.

This is exemplified by the story of a happy couple living in Yorkshire, in the north of England, United Kingdom. For several years, they embarked on the business of manufacturing and distribution of cosmetics products (soaps). Initially they were so successful that they managed to get a contract with a big cosmetic retailer with huge presence in the United Kingdom. To their amazement, the retail company they supplied demanded to procure the rights to the recipes that were used to prepare the soaps for a hefty sum of nine million pounds. As one would expect, the couple were delighted and excited at the same time so they agreed and proceeded to complete the deal.

Surprisingly, a few months after affixing their signatures to the deal of their dreams, they lost all the capital they gained from the sale of the soap recipes. When asked, it was revealed that the couple had invested the entire sum in a new venture, which was generating a loss of £1 in postage expenses. Consequently, instead of profiting, they were operating in the red, simply because they had thought that, should they sell the items in huge quantities, the postage costs would be covered by the huge volume of sales they expected. To their dismay, this wasn't the case. To shorten the story, they simply lost all of their initial investment and were forced to start all over again with no capital in the bank. According to their testimony, it was a difficult learning curve and depressing to accept at times.

However, had they employed some due diligence and done their homework properly before investing based on the economics of scale model (which turned out to be the wrong model for their type of business) they would have been able to steer clear of such a disastrous ending.

In your success journey, having a strategy and the awareness of failure and likely obstacles can greatly multiply your chances of attaining your target goal. These two interconnecting factors can determine your probability of succeeding in a particular venture, even before you embark on it. In fact, no multinational organization on earth can survive and remain competitively sound without a strategy and putting measures in place to negate unforeseen challenges (or failures). Now, on an individual level, to have a strategy is to have a written 'action plan' on how you will execute and achieve your future goals. Because, "*a man without a strategy is akin to drifting ship without a destination.*"

So, if you don't already have a concrete plan for your career, relationship or future, then it is never too late to produce one. Ask yourself these questions. Am I on the right track? What are my goals, passion and desires? Is this where I deserve to be? How can I get to my place of comfort and fulfilment? What is stopping me from accomplishing my goals? What is my five years projection? Is my current path right for me? Could I do better? What are my unique skills? Are the people around me aiding or hindering my progress? Do I possess the will to act on my dreams? These are just some of the life changing questions that most people fail to ask themselves today. Instead, they accept the situation in which they find themselves and often settle for mediocrity and wallow in pettiness.

But it doesn't have to be so because our fear and reluctance to reassess our circumstances is one of the reasons why most people are unhappy, unfulfilled and unsuccessful today. Thus if you find yourself in this category, it is high time you modify your thoughts and start planning your way to your rightful place of limitless success, wellbeing and fulfilment.

> *"It is indeed true that, changes only come to those who make the conscious decision to first seek it and begin to challenge themselves to think of different strategies to bring them to their dream place."*

Furthermore, it is imperative to have it at the back of our minds that the journey to success is not an easy adventure. It requires hard work and the ability to handle challenges. Without this mindset, failure is inevitable. However, your perseverance and mental fortitude to stay the course, irrespective of the amount of failings (challenges) you encounter, would determine how far you can go and, ultimately, how much you accomplish in future endeavours. In fact, by experiencing multiple failures, though not pleasant, helps us to develop the mental strength and strength of character to handle future challenges. Simply put, failure is just one of out of many prices we pay for success and fulfilment. Today, many well-to-do entrepreneurs can attest to this fact.

Another price you pay in exchange for success is loneliness. While some may view this as a big deal, many simply come to terms with it and march on. Well, I see it as a necessity and nothing to worry about, because the path to success is one that you have to walk on your own. Personally, I can vividly recall being enrolled onto my first degree at Kingston University London, and having to relocate far away from my area of residence which was in a particularly deprived area (Peckham) of London (south of England). The feeling I experienced was that of total liberation and the notion that my movement was no longer going to be dictated by my mother.

However, after arriving at the university, as days and months went by, I began to feel what most teenagers would have felt after making such a big move away from all they knew. Immediately, I was embraced by reality, since this sudden change in my environment meant that I could no longer associate with most of my teenage friends. Well, you can call it good fortune, but, admittedly, I was glad that I did relocate, as this helped to broaden my horizon and exposed me to the possibilities outside my comfort zone. To tell you the truth, at the time, most of my friends were on the streets of London, engaging in unruly activities to which I didn't subscribe.

As I progressed from the first to the final year of study, I made new friends along the way, which eased my feeling of 'separation anxiety'. Many years later, I came to understand the reasons why most of my friends from my teenage years drifted away. One of the reasons was that it was part of the process to propel me to my expected place of fulfilment (graduation) at that stage of my journey. You may not understand it now, but nature (God) has some uncanny ways of guiding you to your destiny and be sure that those who are not suppose to be part of your success journey will naturally be shifted away.

Last, but not least, servitude is a paramount component of the process of success and is part of the price we all eventually pay for our accomplishments, whether we like it or not. This is because nobody begins life with millions of pounds in their bank accounts, except those fortunate enough to be born into a wealthy family or given a huge inheritance. In reality, every experience in life is gained through learning and we all learn through different means of which servitude is one of them.

To gain a better understanding of how businesses operate, you have to begin by working in a particular industry and serve others.

In fact, successful entrepreneurs such as Richard Branson (CEO of Virgin), Peter Jones (Technology entrepreneur), Phillip Green (CEO of Acadia group) who owns Top Shop, Dorothy Perkins and BHS, Sir Alan Sugar, Bill Gates and others, started out by 'serving' others. After reading their individual stories, I began to understand the challenges they have had to overcome to get to where they are today.

Indeed, it is true that the experiences we gain from different situations helps to sharpen our character, aptitude and ability to tackle the many complexities of life. Moreover, through servitude, we often pick up subtle skills that will aid us in managing money, profits and people in which ever organization we find ourselves in the future.

It shouldn't come as a shock to you as to why the companies of today generally seek for candidates with a long list of prior experience in a specified field of interest. It is simply the belief that the skill sets obtained over a number of years of 'servitude' could ultimately increase the fortunes of existing businesses. In addition, as you become more experienced, you attract higher remunerations which means more success in all.

Although there are many other things that you would ultimately lose and challenges you would encounter along that narrow path to success, it is important to remain focused on your goals, think of why you embarked on that journey in the first instance and remain steadfast in your quest for success, fulfilment and happiness.

## Motivation for Seeking Success

There are a multitude of reasons why many individuals strive for success and indeed most would do almost anything to attain it, even if it may eventually lead to their detriment. Interestingly, in any area of your life, the level of success accomplished is commensurate to the level of drive, sacrifices and passion invested. In other words, how bad you want something, determines how quickly you get there. Apparently, for many today, the origin of their unrelenting desires to continuously seek for ways to enhance their status, lies in their upbringing. Moreover, it is often discovered that people with such a mindset tend to attract higher paying jobs, promotions and accolades than their peers. This is simply because their drive and desires creates a heightened state of competitiveness which fuels many achievements.

Although our desire for success seems to be an potent motivation factor, for many in our society greed comes very much into play. Whatever your opinion may be, this is a universal truth or else why would a wealthy business mogul want to vociferously amass more riches on top of the vast amount they already possess, if greed is not their motivation? I am not saying that to be greedy is wrong, after all, no one wants to live in a state of penury.

In other cases, jealousy can be the motivation for our betterment. For example, I once lived a few doors away from a couple who didn't have much in the way of cars and other luxurious items, but were seen to be hard working. However, things were about to change. In the space of a few months, the husband gained promotion into a more senior role at his workplace and so did his wife. Then two Ferrari cars suddenly appeared on their driveway and the mortgage on their house was supposedly paid off.

Upon seeing the new improvement in their status, I was admittedly jealous, because I wished I had what they had accomplished. This I considered to be a healthy type of jealousy which motivated me to want to better my situation even more and to arrive at my place of fulfilment. I realised that more creative ideas were needed. From that day onwards, I made a promise to attain the highest degree I could and one day set up a multinational company. Therefore, I urge you to use other people's success as a motivation to catapult yourself to even greater heights.

Despite the roles that desires, passion, greed and jealousy plays in orchestrating success, there are other more subtle factors which are often ignored. Based on personal experience and research, I came to the conclusion that the calibre, mentality and social status of our immediate family members, relatives, friends and the environment in which we grew up from childhood, all have a more profound influence on our hunger for increased achievements. This

I discovered during conversations with some notable entrepreneurs.

Surprisingly, most did not graduate from secondary school simply because they either behaved badly in class or could not concentrate at all or assimilate the concepts that they were presented with. In other accounts, some discovered that they had some innovative business ideas or a flair for business and decided to pursue them further. Consequently, people such as Peter Jones, Sir Alan Sugar, Bill Gates, Steve Job, amongst others, are highly successful. Although, their backgrounds were not so rosy, as many are led to believe, they were able to transform their negative experiences into positive achievements.

Certainly, in my case, my upbringing did influence my passion of higher attainments in my career and future endeavours. The majority of the early stages of my childhood years were spent in a small village in west Africa, where I had lots of fun memories swimming with my brother in the local river, waking up very early to do some house chores, walking long footpaths to primary school, picking up used plastics, bottles and metal cans from the rubbish dump in order to make some quick money for food. Sometimes, the situation was so severe that starvation became the order of the day.

As if that was not severe enough, the breakup of my parents' marriage meant that I and my brother had to move from one location to another to reside under the supervision of abusive relatives. Undoubtedly, my experience of persistent maltreatment adversely impacted my personality. In fact, I suffered from very low self-esteem, speech impairment, reclusiveness and poor performance in school. Perhaps, the instability of life and the breakdown of my parents' marriage was too much to bear at such an innocent age.

Luckily, for me, good fortune came my way. I was lucky to be taken in by my uncle to live with him in the city. It was this God-sent individual who nurtured, impacted a lot of knowledge in me and rejuvenated my inborn self-belief and self-confidence. For me, this was the end of enduring the agony of living under constant fear and pain. For once in my life, I had a renewed hope for a brighter future. Suddenly, the reality of the situation dawned on me and I quickly realised that it was not going be smooth sailing at this stage of my life. In fact, during enrolment into the second half of my secondary education, I was not accepted since I failed to pass the first half of my former secondary education, due to my traumatic experiences. Unfortunately, this meant that I had to start over again.

Despite the disappointment I felt within myself, I forged ahead and used that failure as a motivation to succeed. Day and night, I made it a point of duty to invest a great deal of time studying and revising. Eventually, my hard work paid off and I became a straight 'A' student, served as prefect in my class and, ultimately, as the acting head boy of the entire school. A few years later, I was able to complete three degrees (including, a PhD) in some the world's most prestigious institutions. To me, this is a victory and I have continued to help others by using my experiences as a motivation for greater accomplishments.

Therefore, no matter where your inspiration and motivation for success emanates from, the most important thing is to ensure that you remain resolute and focused on your target goals.

## Reasons Why People Fail to Succeed in Life

In spite of all our hard work, sleepless nights and the unsociable hours invested in a particular pursuit, in the majority of cases, it was discovered that most were not sufficiently equipped with the right knowledge and informed comprehension of the underlying issues surrounding their inability to arrive at their goals and their dream place. Unbeknown to people who suffer such faith, the answer to this mind-boggling question is sometimes simplistic and may be right in front of them, if only they had done their homework properly before starting.

Obviously, when it comes to failure, everyone, including those that are highly educated and those that aren't, can all fall prey to it. Therefore, there is no such thing as an exemption, when it pertains to failure, because, in its absence, success would not exist and thus have no bearing on our lives.

After observing and speaking to entrepreneurs, career hungry individuals and layabouts, I have deduced three fundamental reasons why success still eludes many today. The first is simply an apparent lack of 'will' to want to effect positive changes, followed by their inability to think outside the box and procrastination. To elaborate further, one of the first steps to success is to cultivate a desire to want to change your circumstances for good. It may be that you are unsatisfied with your current job, due to its monotonous or stagnant nature. Such feelings can awaken thoughts of novel and potentially profitable business ideas or strategies that are likely to get you up the promotional ladder within the company.

In many cases, especially in failed businesses, the reasons for their downfall may be due to the fact that they have stopped thinking of innovative ideas that would give them a competitive edge over similar competitors. For others, their issues may be related to replication of existing business, lack of strategy and inadequate execution. As a matter of fact, a lot of traders, especially those in the developing economies, survive on replication of business ideas and do not think outside the box. Yet when their businesses collapse, they blame it on misfortune. So, for any idea or business pursuit to be successful and stand the test of time, innovation has to be at the epicentre of its strategy.

Furthermore, it is not advisable to have a brilliant idea and sit on it (procrastinate) without taking concrete actions to bring it to fruition. No matter how complex or simplistic your ideas may be, they can be achieved, depending on how quickly you are able to put them into motion. Nonetheless, I have heard people blame their unwillingness to transform their ideas into reality on the lack of capital. This is a widespread and lazy excuse which should not be seen as a hindrance at all.

As a matter of fact, most multinational corporations, such as, Apple, Microsoft, Samsung, Hewlett Packard, Sony, Blackberry, Pioneer and the like were not built in a single day and with billions of dollars to begin with. Their ascension to prominence took many years of continued investment, timely (not procrastinated) strategy and adherence to changing trends.

In recent times I have found myself in this similar situation, whereby I had an innovative business idea to supply certain technologies to West Africa. I had very little funds to purchase some initial samples to showcase to potential clients. Although it wasn't easy, I remained resolute and, instead of neglecting the idea, I proceeded to invest the little I had on the prototypes that could be afforded. This is what I mean by 'taking action' and desisting from postponing a potential gold mine.

Many dreams have gone down the drain due to persistent procrastination. Because, while you are busy pondering on the possibilities of your ideas yielding fruits (wealth) or if you can even start in the first instance, someone somewhere may have already began to initiate those ideas and be harvesting huge profits as a result.

It is indeed true that success is relative. In other words, its interpretation differs according to our individual ideology and perception of life. For instance, success to a person that is experiencing severe and recurring migraine could be to find a lasting cure to ease its excruciating symptoms. While, for an impoverished family, being able to get a single meal a day could suffice. If you have ever lived in or visited a third world country, you can best relate to the latter scenario. The truth of the matter is that, some people may be failing to succeed monetarily, yet attain what is success to them in other areas of their life.

Perhaps, an individual who grew up in unimaginable opulence, attended an elite private school and the best institutions the world has to offer and had been handed all he/she ever wished for on a platter of gold may be unfamiliar with the concept of failure (or poverty). For such an individual, the probability of attaining success is significantly higher if due diligence is applied to the wealth inherited.

Similarly, if you reside in an affluent neighbourhood full of accomplished and influential personalities, the calibre of people you encounter and associate with daily would be of similar grandeur. In this situation, your thoughts would be subconsciously influenced and shaped by the lifestyle of these people. A child who finds him or herself in such environment would quickly develop the desire to want to succeed to the levels of the people they are surrounded by. This minimises any possibility of self-doubt and, ultimately failure.

On the other side of the spectrum, if you were unfortunate to have resided or grown up in a poor neighbourhood, like myself, then you will find yourself at an immediate disadvantage. This does not insinuate that those living in deprived neighbourhoods are any less driven or hard working than their counterparts in the more prosperous suburbs.

My point of view is that, in most cases I have observed so far, it is often difficult to break out of the mentality derived from witnessing daily drug dealings, fraudsters, people doing menial jobs, high numbers of joblessness, dysfunctional families, kids with absent fathers, high numbers of single parents, teenagers with unruly behaviours, ghetto English accents (misconstrued for the Queen's English), high proportion of stabbings, gang culture, senseless post code wars, high rate of school dropouts, people with meaningless University certificates and individuals (both old and young) just standing on the streets doing nothing.

Growing up in the above situations is indeed very challenging, but, its impact on future aspirations varies from person to person. For me, in spite of my poor background and difficulties experienced while growing up, I was able to use it as a positive driving force to attain the highest position I could in my line of expertise. My dream was to accomplish significantly more than my peers and parents. I found solace in education as the key to unlock success and prominence. After successfully attaining three University degrees, including a PhD, I continually hungered for more success. This motivated me to begin utilising the skills and expertise I have gained over the years to develop businesses in emerging markets and to help others achieve their full potential.

Unfortunately, for some of my supposed friends, the story was different. Most were caught up in the moment and therefore ended up in jobs which paid very little and others took on some less glamorous career paths, to say the least. After many years, I noticed that their failures were anchored in their inability to see beyond the present and quickly move on from mediocrity. For a minority of them, I surmised that, after all, that was all they ever knew from birth and due to their lack of exposure and enlightenment; they chose to conform instead of embracing positive changes. Therefore, to some extent, they cannot be blamed for having such dismal perception of life and low achievements.

Whether we succeed or fail depends on our individual decisions and choices in life. As children, we are taught different things in school and we also learn a great deal from our parents, relatives and friends. Nonetheless, there comes a point in your existence when a transformation or renaissance appears, and your inability to embrace it will inadvertently lead to significant failures, lack of fulfilment and persistent depression in your life.

## Secret Keys to Effect Success

In this era of economic and social depression, all we see around us are people walking with various burdens, unrealised dreams and aspirations. Many aspire to success or envisage where they want to be in life, but lack the knowledge and mind-power to carry them through to the next level. Dear friend, the truth of the matter is that there is no one magical formula that governs success, because what works for you may not suit another. As the saying goes, *"different strokes for different folks."*

No matter what your achievements are to date, there is still room for improvement. And if you hope to transform your situation for generations to come, then you need to equip yourself with these secret keys that will bring about limitless success, contentment and fulfilment in your life.

In life, there are set principles which orchestrate the order of things that be. Unfortunately, success, fulfilment, happiness and contentment are not exempted from these principles, which we all have to be aware of and adhere to. For instance, in order to gain employment, you have to begin by searching, tendering an application and, if found suitable, you are invited for an interview. Moreover, if successful, you are employed. As you can see, there is a process involved here and it is one that we all have to go through in different areas of our lives, albeit in different forms.

Now, here are 13 powerful keys that if applied will change your life forever and bring your assured success, fulfilment and hopefully, happiness.

### 1 Develop Life-changing Ideas.

This is very important, especially if you are entrepreneurially inclined. Find somewhere quiet, begin to think of different ideas and visualise them in your mind. Ask yourself questions like, are these ideas innovative enough to positively impact people's lives. are they realistic and implementable, and so on.

No matter how crazy, odd or simplistic your ideas may be, remember, that it could change the course of history for ever. For instance, who would have thought that when the prototype of a controllable airplane was first introduced by the Wright Brothers (Orville and Wilbur) in 1903, that it would evolve to become the benchmark for all future, more complex and powerful airplanes which embark on innumerable transatlantic journeys. Interestingly, brainstorming brings about ideas that you never thought were at all possible. It will change your life for the better, so invest time in this practice.

### 2 Setting Goals, Vision and Plan.

This is perhaps the most interesting tool for success. It is not enough to have a brilliant idea, you need to learn to set tangible goals, envision where you want to be in the next five years and then devise a well streamlined plan on how you hope to execute your goals and visions.

> **"A man without a goal, vision and plan, is like a peripatetic ship with no set destination."**

Most people when asked about their future aspirations are often too quick to say that they have it all worked out in their minds. This is mere fallacy and unrealistic. Invest in a pen and a diary and begin to annotate your goals, visions and plans, with specific dates included. This way, you automatically become accountable to yourself. In addition, this will serve as an important motivational tool and a barometer to check your achievements to date.

### 3    Identify you Talents, Passion and Desire.

Most people fail to succeed because they are too lazy to zero in on their God-given talents, passions, desires. Believe it or not, we were all born with peculiar gifts (or talents) which, if not identified and nurtured early in life, can be lost and may take an individual years to re-invigorate. In the world today, people with unique talents have discovered fame, wealth and success. Examples abound, from musicians, inventors, educators, public speakers, right through to athletes.

Now ask yourself, what is that single thing that gives me satisfaction? It could be a job, trade, or any other activity. If you are able to answer this important question, then you have identified your 'passion'. The latter does not lead to exhaustion or lowliness, rather it enriches your life. When you engage your passion, you wake up every morning with an inner happiness in knowing that you are doing something that you enjoy doing. Your passion will bring you unmatched satisfaction and success.

Finally, you need to pinpoint your desires. You may desire a better life, career, wife, six figure salary, beautiful family, a mansion in the countryside, owning your own business and more. The truth of the matter is that we all have desires in life and our desires stretch us that bit further. Therefore, success demands a burning desire. How bad you want it will determine how quickly you are able to achieve those dreams and aspirations you envision.

### 4 Cultivate Self-believe, Self-confidence and Self-determination.

It is brilliant to have ideas, a passion and even mind-blowing talents, but in the absence of the above qualities, failure is the only recourse. For instance, if you want to start a new business and don't have the belief, confidence and determination to make it happen, then you shouldn't expect potential investors to buy into it. No matter what people say about you, what is important is that you have the right attitude and a high opinion of yourself. Otherwise, the confidence and belief you've developed over the years will be stifled and, as a result, you relinquish all hopes of pursuing your dreams and attaining success.

### 5 Take Action and Rebuff Procrastination.

It is disastrous to have a plan and simply shelve it. Many dreams, hopes and aspirations, have gone down the drain as a result. In the majority of cases, they have been too lazy or too busy to act on them. Instead, they simply procrastinate and say, 'I will do it later' or 'when I have enough money to do it'. If you are among this group of people, then you need a wake-up call, quit from that 'I will do it later syndrome' and take action now, not tomorrow. As the saying goes "*a journey of a thousand mile begins with a single step.*" So, why not start by taking small steps, plan! plan! plan! and find solace in the knowledge that success is within reach.

### 6 Transformational Changes.

Most people have stopped growing in their careers, businesses and other endeavours, simply because they have become over complacent, too comfortable and unwilling to embrace changes that will make a huge contribution to their lives. Moreover, on closer assessment, it is discovered that many have exhausted all avenues available to them and others have stopped dreaming or dreaming big. In these cases, the remedy is to adopt positive transformation or re-invention of one's self.

To get out of stagnancy in your life, you need to do something new. In other words, you need to let go of the old you and let the current you die for a new you to emerge. For a seed to yield fruit, it must first die. In addition, according to an old adage, *"if a caterpillar does not know how to be transformed into a butterfly, it will forever remain in that state."*

Therefore, for you to find success, you need to change the old ways of doing things and undergo metamorphosis. Because, if you keep doing things the old way, don't expect to obtain a different result. Therefore, reinvent yourself, be creative and think of things you can do differently that will get you your desired and expected results (success).

*7 Find and Define your True Purpose.*

It is indisputable that your purpose and success, are intertwined and success brings fulfilment. Without a defined purpose, you can never be successful or contented. Many fail to succeed because they find themselves stuck in careers that were not meant for them, studied university courses with no true intention to work in their chosen field, replicating businesses and mimicry, not knowing that the purpose for which they were designed may lie in an entirely different pathway.

Thus it is important to quit following other's footsteps and focus on discovering your God-given purpose in life. The bottom line is that all humans were created with one mission and that is to fulfil our individual purpose.

Furthermore, your true purpose could be in a hidden talent that, when displayed, attracts a lot of commendations, perhaps a flair for business, invention, knowledge impartation, coaching, mentoring or a sporting activity. Believe me, when you find your defined purpose, then you will be at peace with yourself. Things begin to unravel in an unexpected fashion and, above all, you begin to multiply in almost magical ways. Always remember that in your purpose lies the key to prosperity and lasting contentment.

## 8 Will Power and Winners Attitude.

Do you possess the will and the right attitude that will bring you results in all your endeavours? Or do you simply wait on others to do it for you, whilst sitting and doing nothing? As the saying goes, "*you can take a horse to the stream, but, you cannot force it to drink.*" In other words, you can have a dream or a fantastic idea, but don't possess the will to bring it to fruition.

The truth is that, if you wait on others, yours dreams will never be realised. In addition, always foster a positive attitude ('I can, I will, I am and I deserve') and be willing to invest your time and effort in order to achieve all your desires.

## 9 Influential Associations and Connections.

The people you associate and connect with the most will inevitably influence your adopted style and quality of life. Moreover, whether you become successful or not will depend on their level of accomplishments. Therefore, it is imperative to make connections with highly reputable individuals (role models) and those who will impact positivity and the right ingredients of success in you.

Now, list the ten closest and most influential people (father, mother, brothers, sisters, spouses, friends, aunties, uncles, cousins, neighbours and personalities of interest) in your life.

From your candid assessment of their lives, are they successful? Are they career oriented and focused? What nature of jobs are they involved in? Are they proactive or idle? Do they possess a positive outlook on life? Do their lifestyles motivate you to want to better yourself? Are their lifestyles worth emulating? Do they possess characteristics that draw great admiration from other people? Are they outstanding in their various fields? If you cannot answer these questions favourably for all ten, then you need to identify who amongst these individuals are the odd ones out and immediately disassociate yourself from them.

The reason being that, by anchoring yourself to progressive and influential individuals, you will be motivated and challenged to want to do better in all your personal life. In other words, a blind man cannot lead one with a clear vision. Losers will always pull you down both mentally and physical and this is what you least need if success is your ultimate goal.

### 10 Adopt an Opportunist Mindset.

A talented entrepreneur is one who is able to spot an opportunity and pursue it obsessively. On the other hand, an entrepreneurial genius is one with the foresight to identify potential where others envision failure. As the saying goes, *"opportunity comes but once in a lifetime."*

Today, most people, especially, the so called 'youths' will never be successful and accomplished, because they are distracted, lazy, too comfortable doing those things that will never bring them fulfilment in their lives. Opportunities abound, but you have to be willing to seek and embrace those that are available to you. Think like an inventor who constantly seek innovative ways of doing things and, as result, devises products that you and I never thought were at all possible. This is the opportunist mindset and one we all need to embrace, because success cannot be obtained by mere coincidence.

## 11 Dream Big.

One of the biggest decapitators of success is setting the bar too low. Never put a compromise on your dreams, otherwise you will always attain very little in life. It is okay to dream, but, what is important is how ambitious those dreams are. Many people today are walking dead because they have stopped dreaming. Maybe you are feeling too complacent, because you drive that nice car you purchased on credit, live in a plush, but rented or mortgaged apartment, go on holidays with the little savings you were able to amass over a number of months and work in an okay paying job. If you find yourself in this category, then you are living in a delusional lifestyle, because the day you fail to honour one or more of your payments, your properties are repossessed. This is not what living a dream life entails.

Big dreamers think big and make big strides to achieve them. Living a dream is about independence and fulfilment. For example, owning your own profitable business debt-free, buying a house and a car outright, sponsoring your children to the best private institutions without feeling burdensome, having the luxury of going on vacation whenever you wish, spending on those things you fancy, waking up in the morning and playing golf or fixing up the garden, without fear of where your next meal will come from and others, are just some of the dreams I am referring to. Therefore, I encourage you to dream big and take proactive steps to achieve them.

## 12 Mentoring and Coaching.

Most people who succeed in life are those who proactively seek mentors and coaches to help make their ambitions, goals and plans more meaningful. It is not enough to have a brilliant idea, but, how you go about executing them to get the best results. This is why effective coaching and mentorship comes highly recommended. By doing this, certain pitfalls can be averted; be it in your chosen career direction or in an area of business. In addition, you are presented with tangible steps and clarity of vision, which can only lead to you to success.

*13 Seek God Almighty First.*

This may not seem apparent or logical to those that are of no religious persuasion. In my life, I have witnessed the advantages of embarking on a journey with God's consent. As a young man preaching in Sunday schools and praying diligently to my Creator (God Almighty) for success, I have obtained great rewards as a result.

Your success to date and others to come has the hallmarks of God's mighty intervention written all over them, but as imperfect humans we are often too quick to credit it all to our own flawed wisdom and mental prowess. Not knowing that there is supreme God who orchestrates all things for our common good.

Dear reader, God has purposed you for bountiful success, fulfilment and happiness, if only you would seek him today. To confirm this, He urged us through the Holy Scriptures that we should; "*seek first the kingdom of God and His righteousness; and all these things shall be added unto us.*" (Matthew 6:33, NKJV)

Thus, to accomplish anything in life, your first point of call should be to seek His intervention. This is an act with great reward attached to it. What more, in the book of Matthew 7:7, it is stated with great emphasis that we should, "*ask and it will be given to you; seek and you will find; knock and the door will be opened to you.*" Remember that true and lasting success can only be obtained from God Almighty, so why not seek him today and watch your life transform to a level that you least expect.

It is indeed true that we were all born with the liberty to seek success, fulfilment and happiness. However, these three wishes that all humans strive for, cannot come to fruition without hard work, diligence and an intricate comprehension of the prerequisite knowledge of some governing principles, as highlighted above.

I hope that in your current situation, you will seize the opportunity to utilise the tools herein to help carve your path towards the light at the end of your tunnel of failures and challenges. Success is a difficult and treacherous journey, full of many unknowns that only the prudent at heart can navigate. Therefore, believe in yourself, in your capabilities and trust God to lead you to your place of unlimited success.

# 5

# Immerse Yourself To Achieve

*"He who busies himself with things other than improvement of his own self, becomes perplexed in darkness and entangled in ruin. His evil spirits immerse him deep in vices and make his bad actions seem handsome."*

*Ali ibn Abi Talib*

In this day and age, the upheavals, uncertainties and sufferings witnessed around the world, have presented many individuals with various challenges. Not least, the state of the global economy and rampant abuse of leadership in the corridors of power, where the less privileged are left with very little room to manoeuvre, and are impoverished.

Sometimes I wonder why things (inequality and unfairness) are the way they are in our society today and wish that, perhaps, in a different time and place, things could be a little different, with a more advantageous and positive outlook for those who fall victim to such hurtful vices that we have become acquainted to.

Be that as it may, it is no surprise that many people who find themselves in such indigence and disadvantaged positions in life are often ambitious in their quest for betterment, greatness and a swift riddance from their often unsatisfactory economic posture. Today, a high proportion of these individuals still vie with great zeal for wealth, success, happiness, and fulfilment in their lives. Sadly, it is a sorry realisation that some are often too reluctant and lackadaisical in their strides to take those pertinent steps that will get them to that place they have dreamt of and envisioned for so long.

Others, are simply prolific losers, often drowned in negative thoughts and will never achieve anything of significance in their lives, because they have continued to fail to move from their place of comfort to a place of new and sustainable opportunities.

I am aware that you, a close relative, spouse, or associate of yours, may find themselves in such situation. Quit worryingly, it is my belief that the situation in which you find yourself this very minute is ever meant to remain permanent. The only thing that is permanent is life is change. But you have to want that change to happen in your life and, above all, you have to conjure the courage to want to do what it will take to get you out of the place you find yourself today. Only then will you begin to see lasting positive transformations in both your once dysfunctional economic and social status.

Now, you may ask, what is this process that I have to go through to get me to where I want to be in my life? This is a valid question that many people ask themselves today and it may surprise you how simplistic the answer may be. As you are aware, no city in the world was built in a single day and out of nothing. In a similar fashion, the wealthy and those who occupy the upper echelons of our society did not simply wake up one day and discover themselves in such state of magnanimous opulence. There is a popular adage which states that "*the mechanic that would perfect his work, must first sharpen his tools.*"

In the same light, if you must experience a tectonic shift in your situation, you have to comprehend one simple principle that will change your life forever. I once attended at a secondary school in in Nigeria, West Africa, whose dictum was "*hard work for success.*" For many years I had this somewhat short and powerful sentence deeply etched at the back of my mind and I took it wherever I went.

At first, it did not occur to me how impactful it would turn out to be. But, as I approached adulthood and became wiser to the secrets of life and success, it (the dictum) began to manifest in different areas of my life. Not least in the area of educational pursuits and business excellence. Today, this has turned out to be one of the most important driving force that has continued to propel me to greater heights and achievements in life.

## The Process of Immersion Made Clear

Believe it or not, in life, nothing is given to you on a platter of gold. We all have to strive tirelessly, by way of 'hard work, unflinching focus, perseverance and relentless determination', if we are to attain anything tangible out of the university of life. But, beside these, there is one single action that we all must embrace if we are truly serious about transcending from a place of mediocrity to one of plentiful success, and where our desires materialise.

Dear friend, the answer to your problem is 'immersion.' The later is described in the Oxford dictionary as a deep mental involvement in something. In order words, it is a process of engaging oneself in a particular activity to bring about a desired outcome. Therefore, it comes as a surprise and yet baffling that most people do not indulge in this simple practice very often. Perhaps the lack of awareness and knowledge of it may be responsible or could it be that we have become mentally blinded by certain enticements and preoccupied by the ever growing distractions we are presented with today? As the American educator, Daniel Greenburg quoted;

*"If you watch young children play, you will notice that they create games, characters, situations, whole worlds in which they immense themselves with intense concentration."*

Ponder on the above quote for a minute. Is this of any meaning to you? Or is he telling us to behave more like children? Far from it. What he meant was that we should search within and, above all, be creative by immersing ourselves in the world we envisage, and our dreams. You can liken this to a mechanic preparing his tools, before starting the process of fixing a mechanical fault. You too can do the same today to better your situation. Therefore, if you want the following;

1. To become a successful musical genius, then you must immerse yourself in the art of music. Work on your talent and perfect your artistry to be appreciated by others.

2. To become a doctor (medical or otherwise), then immerse yourself in those things that will help you to obtain that goal and get a mentor who would guide you through the process involved.

3. To become a prominent politician, immerse yourself in the field of politics, up to the point of drowning (not literally). How bad you want something will determine how much work and time you dedicate to it.

4. To become a business tycoon, immerse yourself in developing unique ideas and proactively transform those ideas into working ideas and not mere 'idle hopes'. Ideas that will impact positively on people's lives will bring you great fortune and change your life for the better. Study the ropes, do your research and learn from the mistakes of similar businesses. Assess why they failed or succeeded in the end.

5. To become a public speaker, immerse yourself in the act of public speaking. Go to public speaking classes and associate with people of like minds. And in your quest, learn to immerse yourself in consistent practising and, when the opportunity presents itself, always volunteer to deliver a speech, no matter how small the audience may be.

6. To be promoted to higher positions in your work place, you have to immerse yourself in hard work and continuing professional development activities. You have to do something extraordinary to achieve more than you are achieving at the moment. The truth of the matter is that the man or woman ahead of you may have already be doing or have done something

that you are not aware of. So do your best to discover what it is or the process they had to go through in order to gain such promotion. In all, do not embark on anything that will prove detrimental to your person.

7. To lead a happy and healthy lifestyle, fervently pursue those things that you desire or for which you have leanings. Immerse yourself in those things that will bring you joy and a better state of health.

8. To develop and maintain a long lasting relationship, you must first search within and do your homework on the qualities you desire in a prospective partner, because the state of your relationship has a strong correlation with your personality and behaviour. I am not pretending to be a relationship coach myself, but wisdom has no boundaries. Have you ever wondered why the relationship of most married couples do not work out? It is mostly because, from the onset, either the basis of their relationship was to do with lust or the wrong intentions. Had they exercised due diligence, the outcome could have been different.

9. To become successful, depending on what this means to you, immerse yourself in those activities that will bring you success. Any type of success you seek requires a price and your awareness of this widely ignored truth, especially amongst the youth of today, can turn the tide of success in your favour.

Remember, that, *"prominence seeks the brave and not a weakling."* Experience has taught me that to immerse oneself is to be bold and with this boldness you can achieve just about anything you put your mind to. This concept has immensely transformed my career, life, and business pursuits. Moreover, I am not so neglectful of the imperative role that my belief in God Almighty has continued to play in my journey in life. Beloved, I am proud to urge you to first seek Him in all you do and all your desires will be granted in abundance.

# 6

# Embracing Change For Prosperity

*"Change will not come if we wait for some other person or some other time. We are the ones we've been waiting for. We are the change that we seek."*

*President Barak Obama*

The notion of change can be likened to an individual embarking on a new adventure. Although it sounds exciting, he or she still lacks a clear mental picture of the challenges, dangers, duration and eventualities it entails. Just like a tunnel, when you enter from one end you are ignorant of what to expect at the exit. But the only prior knowledge we have of this is that there is usually an opening unto light at the end of any tunnel, which relieves our initial anxiety.

There are moments in life when we find ourselves in situations bearing the hallmarks of discontentment, stagnation and lowliness of mind. In most cases, this could be related to a job (career) which you may find has become monotonous with no prospect of promotion to the next level up, despite all the hard work and long hours that you invest daily. Perhaps, it could be that you are stuck in a non-progressive and abusive relationship, bad state of wellbeing (too fat or obsessed) due to an unhealthy lifestyle, isolation with no friends around you, poor level of achievements, have insecurities (poor self-confidence, self-esteem, self-belief and the like) and don't know where or who to turn to for help, or you are at a point in life where you feel dissatisfied, unappreciated and unfulfilled. Whatever your reasons may be, the truth of the matter is that, as long as the human race exist, there will be the need for changes in various areas of our lives.

If you find yourself in such situations as highlighted above, then it is time to embrace 'change', for without it there is no breakthrough.

> *According to George Barnard Shaw, "progress is impossible without change and those who cannot change their minds, cannot change anything."*

In other words, irrespective of the nature and list of changes you seek in your life today, you need to be aware that it starts with 'you' and your ability to transform your thoughts. Change itself is borne out of a burning "desire and passion" within us and a realisation that we are not where we desperately want to be in life.

You may have heard the saying that, *"a little change can make a big difference."* This is not true and is for the faint hearted and those still reeling in their lackadaisical state of mind. Believe me, if your dream is to experience an exponential shift in your quality of life, then you have to take a bold leap of faith and do something extraordinary.

Recently, a close friend who has been working in a company for 17 years suddenly walked into his manager's office and handed in his work badge and other company properties to facilitate his resignation.

At first I thought that he had gone mad, because he relied heavily on his job to pay his bills. Therefore, to me, he had no valid reason to resign. However, as we conversed further, I discovered that his job had become too routine and, to make matters worse, he had no prospect of being promoted to a new position, despite engaging in company-sponsored continual professional development (CPD) programmes. Truthfully, when you are at your wits end, that is when the change you continually evaded catches up with you.

As luck would have it, this extraordinary step helped him to seek and gain employment in another company in a position which he has been vying for, coupled with a significantly improved pay package. In his case, stagnation, monotony and the unfulfilment of purpose were the catalyst for change.

Be not weary, because when you find yourself at the end of the road and there seems to be no more room to manoeuvre in your current situation, this is enough to kick start that desire for changes that will bring you to your dream place and realisation of your true potential.

## The Will to Initiate Change

Today, very few people tend to seek changes for a brighter future, while others simply cannot find the impulsion to conceive the thought of changing their current status, even if they are apparently not satisfied with it. In the majority of cases, this same set of individuals consistently complain to family members and close associates about the magnitude of their discontentment and how they wish their lousy state would magically improve.

Surprisingly, in many established social and economic structures, today, the idea of change scares the living daylight out of the them and suddenly, they become needlessly anxious. The truth is that, change is healthy and you can never have too much of it.

The 'will' to change is highly imperative, because, without it, your life will never improve until you conjure the courage to embrace it, and, make it work for you. In doing so, you can begin to look forward to a more properous future.

*As Maya Angelou stated, that, "If you don't like something, change it. If you can't change it, change your attitude."*

What is your attitude to change? Are you one to sit back and hope that it will come to you? Do you work hard enough to bring about the improvements you seek in your situation? Do you believe in working harder or smarter? Have you thought of assessing your situation, in order to identify areas needing change? Where and how do you find the tools to help actualise those changes you seek in your situation? These are some of the many questions that you have to ask yourself from time to time, so as to develop the right attitude and approach to effect positive changes in your life.

Be warned, the number one reason why most people fail to succeed today is due to their inability and unwillingness to implement those positive changes that are felt within, even when the time is right.

The gentleman who suddenly resigned from his job would have been viewed as a loser by many, but he had a higher purpose to fulfil and thus was not comfortable with the 'it pays the bills' type of job he had. This is well summed up by this quote from my hero, President Barak Obama, which states that, *"focusing your life solely on making a buck shows a certain poverty of ambition. It asks too little of yourself. Because it's only when you hitch your wagon to something larger than yourself that you realize your true potential."*

Thus, be brave, bold and courageous in your journey to bettering your situation. Bear no regrets, but embrace thoughtful purpose in all.

## Bringing Changes to Fruition

Now, what do we do with the changes that we have come to know? During the United State presidential election of 2008, the now sitting president, Barack Obama, ran under the slogan of 'change.' This was because he realised the need for a seismic shift in his country's governance, social and economic situations and could see through the eyes of his electors a desperate desire for it.

His belief was that the changes we seek lies within 'us.' For there to be a change in our situation, we have to first rediscover ourselves. You cannot simply sit idle and hope that, that poor status of yours will be transformed overnight. I'm sorry to burst your bubble, it will not happen, not in a million years. The onus is on you to put in the hard work, be patient and persevere.

Take for instance, the corporate world. You may have noticed that companies who often implement changes to their mode of operation, product ideas, services and promotional strategies in line with new trends and the changing lifestyles of potential consumers, are found to be more competitive, highly profitable and survive in difficult economic times. In most cases, these companies have to diversify their product portfolio and be more creative to attract new breed of consumers. In the car industry, manufacturers are faced with the herculean task of varying their range of cars and design to appeal to the younger generation. This is change in motion, in it lies their survival.

Think about this for a moment, why are electronics giants, such as, Apple and Samsung, more profitable than other competitors (Blackberry, Nokia, Motorola and others)? And why do they feel the need to introduce new models of an existing technology within three to six months of launching a previous model? The answer is to stave off competition, by researching and implementing changes in line with the constantly changing trends and the requirements of consumers around the world. Today, most companies invest heavily in customer surveys and other research tools to help determine what changes or modifications are necessary to stay ahead of the competition.

The same should apply to us as individuals. We cannot continue to do things the old way and expect any marked differences in our situation. You must begin by making notable adjustments where needed and, above all, you have to want the change to begin to manifest itself in your life. Be 'proactive, consistent and resilient' in your endeavour to bring about positive changes in your life.

However, it will not happen if you try too hard or move too fast. You have to exercise patience, take things a step at a time, analyse your situation properly, set achievable goals on paper, analyse your goals and try to envisage the end-result. Sometimes, visualising the expected outcomes of the changes you want can serve as an indispensable motivational tool for you to want to initiate that changes in the first instance.

Now, ask yourself questions such as, where do I really want to be? For instance, you may have studied medicine at University, but is really being a medic your true purpose? Can I do better in a different field? Am I truly happy with my current situation? Why am I in this situation and how did I get here in the first place? Can I push myself that extra mile? Will a change solve my problems? This is tantamount to going to the hospital for a routine health check. And by fostering such approach, you are certainly on your way to living a, successful, happy and an accomplished lifestyle.

## Steps to Commence Changes for Success

### Transformation

It is difficult to come by success without a transformation from the old to the new. In other words, for the changes you make today to translate into lasting success, your old self has to first die for the new you to emerge.

> *As the popular British author, Clive Staples Lewis, stated, that, "it may be hard for an egg to turn into a bird: it would be a jolly sight harder for it to learn to fly while remaining an egg. We are like eggs at present. And you cannot go on indefinitely being just an ordinary, decent egg. We must be hatched or go bad."*

Transformation of oneself, in terms of your character, image and mindset, is the key to attaining success. As highlighted in the above quote, you cannot stay in your comfort zone or keep doing things the old way and expect any difference in your life. Rather, we have to break away from the norm and be transformed. For a seed to germinate and bring forth new fruits, it must first die. Therefore, you can either remain in a shell of 'just a little will do' and suffer or embrace positive transformations that will change your life for the better. The choice is yours to make, so chose the latter.

### Procrastination

As the saying by the English poet, Edward Young, goes, *"procrastination is the thief of time."* This is undeniably factual, because for the lazy minded, a little tarry will suffice. But, for those with a vision and the determination to succeed at all cost, a little tarry means a wasted opportunity. Now, which category do you belong? Are you the lazy type or an opportunist? Remember that what you spend every second of every hour of your day doing will determine how much you attain in life. Change your attitude to life today or, otherwise, you will end up losing more than you bargained for.

This is better summarised by Napoleon Hill, when he stated that, *"Procrastination is the bad habit of putting off until the day after tomorrow, what should have been done the day before yesterday."* So why not turn your mindset of inaction into action today. Be more proactive if you have been found wanting in this area of your life. Always remember to take action now, don't wait for another time. If you feel it, pursue it, even when you don't want to. This is the spirit and mindset of a winner. So don't let procrastination steal away your success by not taking on those positives changes that are needed.

Listen to the inner voice. It sometimes baffles me why most people are still in the habit of ignoring their inner instincts. Believe it or not, this is one area, if harnessed fully, will stop your life from falling off the cliff faster than the blink of an eye.

Sometimes, we find ourselves in difficult situations with nowhere to turn, but there is always a silent voice of reasoning within us which always tries to propel us in the right direction. Many times, I have depended on my wisdom in relation to various life-changing choices, but failed woefully. This is simply because I have often refused to adhere to the voice of change within me.

When seeking changes to a situation, very often the answers may be within you. All you have to do is to be more attentive and let the voice of reasoning guide you accordingly. The change you seek is in you and no amount of counselling can influence your decision in the end.

*Re-strategise your strategy*

What do you do in the face of certain failure? Do you simply cave in and forfeit all you've acquired with your years of hard work? Surely not. Re-strategising is an adaptability skill that can turn the tide of failure in your favour. Many times in my life, I have found myself in situations which I thought had no foreseeable solution. In a particular instance, when I graduated from my doctoral studies in 2012, I could not find a job for some months, despite applying to hundreds of employers. To be honest, I was totally disappointed, stressed and anxious about my future. As a result, I began to play the blame game, as anyone in my situation would.

One day, I was telling my story to a friend in a local pub, and in the process, she suddenly said, why don't you become a motivational speak? From that point on, the rest is history. Then, I made a decision to begin giving speeches in conferences, and blogging about various life-changing topics. To my surprise, the response was overwhelming and more positive than I had thought was possible.

That was how I identified and continued developing my motivational speaking prowess.

The point that I am trying to make here, is that, just because you are jobless does not imply that you have to stay that way. Learn a new skill, think of new ideas, be creative, follow your heart and you will surely find success and fulfilment.

*Change position*

Many times, we find ourselves in a location that has all that we've ever wished for and simply stay put. This is what is called our 'comfort zone'. There is nothing wrong with being in this position in your life. However, are you fulfilling your true purpose in that place? If your answer to that is no, then a change is needed.

Why stay in a place where you are clearly comfortable, but happiness still eludes you? Change now and see how fast your desires for success can come through. Be it either a stagnant job, relationship or business, there is always a way out. So, take it upon yourself to implement those changes that will make you happy, fulfilled and successful. After all, you only have one life to live.

*Keep up the momentum*

It is all well and good to implement positive changes in life, but your efforts will become futile if you are unable to sustain them in the end. How do you keep the momentum going? This is imperative, particularly if you have just recently embarked on a journey of change. It could sometimes be daunting and you feel like giving up.

Believe me, if success was easy to come by, then we will all be successful by doing very little. According to the novelist, Arnold Bennett, *"any change, even a change for the better, is always accompanied by drawbacks and discomforts."* Dear friend, I am not saying that it will be easy, but, with persistence, the changes you make today can become sustainable and long lasting.

Whatever your situation, change is inevitable whether you like it or not. However, you may not seek it today, but life surely has a tricky way of throwing up situations that will cause you to continuously reassess your position and status. So, why wait for such times, when you could do it now. Remember, in order to succeed in any area of life, action is key and change should be instinctive.

# 7

# The Contradictions Of Life

*"I tend not to dwell on the parallels between chess and business, chess and the martial arts, or any two things for that matter, because the truth is that all pursuits are connected if we gain an eye for the thematic links."*

*Joshua Waitzkin*

There are innumerable occurrences in life that are sometimes wholly logical to our human comprehension and, at least, at first glance, seem to have nothing more to it than meets the eye. Is this really the case or are we often too reluctant to explore the plethora of probabilities, parallels and contradictions that are set before us?

For me, the quest for both convoluted, ecclesiastical and terrestrial wisdom and knowledge were not mere fascinations, but a fervent daily pursuit. Make no mistake; if you are able to master and apply the act of deciphering the silent codes engraved within the fabric of life, then you have unravelled the true meaning of a competitive advantage. This is akin to adopting a vantage point on a hill in the battle field or like an Eagle with an exceptional sighting ability to pick out a prey from remarkable distances with military precision.

Do you know that all around us are innumerable parallels, which have been deliberately fashioned to ensure equilibrium in the way things operate in the universe? I know that you may be questioning the importance thereof. Well, the answer is simply to aid our comprehension of the reasons why things are the way they are and why some events (tragedies, poverty, dissension, pain, death, failure, illness, wars, amongst others) are inevitable and why no amount of methodical preparation or forecast can avert them.

Perhaps this revelation may not come as a surprise to you. On the contrary, millions of people out there are not so privileged to be enlightened, due to some uncontrollable social, economic or environmental constraints, or probably do not apply themselves enough in the hope of gaining an in-depth knowledge of these incidences and why they occur without forewarning. To them this may appear somewhat revealing.

Do not be weary, in fact nature (God Almighty) has deliberately made it so and only those who are truly gifted with an out-of-this-world knowledge can satisfactorily explicate the logic behind these contradictions and use it to their advantage when presented with difficult situations.

## The Essence of Contradictions

Whether you believe it or not, for as long as we reside under the supernatural laws of God Almighty (irrespective of your religious leanings) and the complex dynamics of the universe, there will always be people who are rich and poor. Successes (attainments, accomplishments, prosperity and achievements) and failures, equality and inequality in all spheres of life, times of war and peace, jealousy and contentment, hatred and love, greed and honesty, fidelity and infidelity, moments of plentiful and famine, periods of recession and prosperity, good and evil, might and weakness, knowledge and ignorance, wisdom and folly, influence and the absence of it, times of sickness and good health, existence and extinction, light and darkness, happiness and sadness, certainty of purpose and confusion, positive and negative, action and reaction (concerning the law karma), perpetuity and limitations, mortality and immortality and many more.

Although, there are many more contradictions that are not mentioned above, it is hoped that you have been able to understand the point I was alluding to. However, it is imperative that you understand these and others that are not immediately apparent to the physical eyes, if you are to progress or obtain success (whatever your interpretation of this may be) in life and distinguish yourself from the naive thinkers present in the world today.

For instance, if you are on a particular course of study, a journey into a new career direction or about to make a life changing decision, this may help you to attain a heightened state of awareness of the unforeseen challenges, pitfalls and obstacles that may be in store for you. Therefore, by familiarising yourself with the understanding of life's contradictions, you are better prepared and equipped to persist on a winning path in all your endeavours.

Many a time, I have experienced this myself and I am just one of the many living proofs out there, that the awareness of the many oppositions or contradictions we observed on a daily basis, if deciphered correctly, can be a game changer and therefore make our experiences in life more meaningful.

After completing my doctoral studies in 2012, I found it quite difficult gaining meaningful employment, despite having the right skill sets for the roles to which I tendered hundreds of applications for. For months on end, the interviews were not forthcoming as expected. It got so bad that I sought help from the social welfare providers that were only too willing to help out with survival funds. This I discovered to be highly depressing, since, up to that period, I had no reason to seek succour from any external source.

However, instead of bowing to the pressures of such dire circumstances, I decided to be creative in a number of ways. One of which was to look into contract work in various marketing companies and start my own entertainment outfit with disk jockey (DJ) as a speciality. In addition, I also thought of delving into the recruitment industry, but later withdrew my interest due to the lack of start-up capital.

In spite of the challenges I encountered, I remained focused and determined to succeed at all cost. This is because my understanding of the contradictions of life helped to pacify the anxiety that resulted from my experience. Interestingly, it was during this period that I discovered my ability to motivate, inspire and empower others to get them out of discontentment and unfulfilment.

Dear friend, if you immerse yourself in the study of the aforementioned contradictions of life and more, then you have a secretly potent weapon that will turn the tide of success in your favour. Because, with this knowledge, I have come to know that there are periods of sufferings (or trials) that we all have to go through for reasons to do with the endurance, fortitude of character and the unveiling of one's true purpose in life. Evidently, during this period, those innate talents and gifts within you surface and, in the absence of other distractions, you begin to devise ways to better harness them.

Remember, that knowledge is power and a gift that stays with you for eternity. Thus, as long as the human race exists, there will always be contradictions and questions like; why do the good die young and not the evildoer? Why am I in this situation and how did I arrive here in the first instance? Is there a way out? Whatever, the case may be, be rest assured that there is no situation that you are presented with that you cannot handle. The key is for you to be aware of the inevitability of many occurrences in life and not to be overwhelmed by them.

# 8

# Identity Crisis And How To Ascertain Yours

*"A man who lacks an identity is akin to a lost ship, drifting away aimlessly without a set destination, or a sea without a definite shore line within reach. He tarrys with intent until he finds his true self."*

*Dr Dickson Aleroh*

When you hear the word identity, what immediately comes to mind? Is it a simple ID card, a passport, a driving licence, or otherwise? Far from it, to me, the issue of a person's identity goes beyond having a printed document in your wallet or handbag. Rather, I like to view an identity simply as the true you. In other words, your identity is who you truly are and that thing from which your qualities and attributes originate. Around the world today are innumerable individuals, especially those approaching adulthood, experiencing difficulties in their lives due to the absence of an identity.

During my childhood years, up to the age of ten, all I knew was a broken home, and a loving father, who was severely ill. Eventually, he gave up the ghost and from that moment onwards, my identity was no longer clear to me. At times, I would look in the mirror, and ask myself, who I really am. The issue got so bad that whenever I find myself in difficult situations, I immediately go into a state of total bewilderment. Consequently, I have often found it difficult to conjure up a reasonable solution to help bring about a meaningful resolution in various instances. For the first time in my life, I felt lost and a sense of grave disappointment in my person. This was when I discovered that I was suffering from an 'identity crisis', and its impact in my life became all the more apparent, as I grew up.

The issue of identity widely resonates amongst most younger folks in many parts of the world today. Especially, in regions where high rates of disconnected families are rife, most teenagers are more predisposed to experiencing a conflict in identity, from on my personal experience.

However, it has become an established fact that every individual grew up or should normally grow up with a peculiar identity, which is usually formed through experimentation with different identities, as they go right from childhood, adolescence, through to adulthood. This acquired identity, when fully formed, may ultimately shape our physical, psychological, and social developmental architectures, when approaching adulthood. As a matter of fact, our identity is so important, that it determines our mannerism, likes and dislikes, the nature of associations and social groups we form, our way of life, and ultimately, our level of success later in life.

Albeit somewhat complex, our identity encompasses the following aspects of life;

1.  Adaptability in situations.
2.  Articulation and diction.
3.  Emotiveness and affection.
4.  Behavioural tendencies (alcohol abuse, misuse of banned substances, sexual impropriety, antisocial behaviours, thieving, bullying, abuse of partners and more).
5.  The choices we make, which pertains to the types of relationships, career pathways, social circle, friendship, our circle of friends and the like.
6.  Confidence and self-esteem.
7.  Mannerism.
8.  Personal drive and level of ambition.

9.   Personal integrity and trustworthiness.
10.  Personality traits.
11.  Social interaction capabilities.
12.  Social and economic status.
13.  Susceptibilities.

Whether you like or not, the lack of a well defined identity affects various areas of our lives and this becomes apparent in different stages of our development. For me, growing up in a small village in Southern Nigeria (Delta state), where age-old traditions and cultural practices overshadow the preservation of certain pivotal and unalienable human rights, most parents and guardians often hide behind the pretext of keeping to the tenets of a rigid and archaic system of nurturing their younger generation by way of abuse disguised as discipline.

Besides the impact of culture and tradition, the environment in which this occurs is also a chief factor in deciding our individual identities. This is because the environment in which a child was brought up would inadvertently play a decisive role in the advanced stages of his or her life.

## How to Find Your Identity

Now, you may be pondering in what your identity truly is? How do you identify yours? From whom do you derive your identity? And, does is matter at all, whether you have it or not? Frankly, these are the questions that often baffles me and I have had to ponder on them many times, especially after the loss of my father at a very tender age. Since then, I have lost almost all mental picture of the man he was. Some of the memories I still recall are of a man who exuded greatness, showed unconditional love, caring, upright, resilient and hardworking without faltering.

In my case, my father was my identity. The latter is defined as a group of characteristics which determines who or what a person is, a close similarity, or something that sets you apart from others. In essence, your identity defines you and brings out some distinctive qualities which can only be attributed to you.

For example, today the epidemic of teenagers standing wastefully on the streets of London and forming a plethora of gangs stems from the fact that they are misunderstood and lack a sense of identity. According to the UK's Office Of National Statistics, it was concluded that, of the recorded 26.4 million households in Britain, 29% were predominantly single parents with dependent children and the figure is set to rise further. Such is the severity of the status quo in families in many parts of the country today.

Moreover, as you may be aware, the majority of children mostly live with their mother after a split occurs and very often they grow up in unhealthy and, sometimes, in unstable circumstances. Particularly, when it pertains to boys, mothers are often not able to control their behaviour as they approach the teenage stages, whereby they become over adventurous in their approach to life.

The truth of the matter is that the absence of a father figure in the lives of both young males and females has continued to create a huge identity crisis in our society. These youths have often resorted to seeking solace through other avenues, such as, gang affiliations, substance abuse and unhealthy grooming by much older individuals with devious intents, to name a few. All these is because of the need to feel a sense of family, security and direction in their lives.

Unbeknown to these youths, who find themselves in such unfortunate circumstances, that the eventualities of such actions may result in criminal convictions, imprisonment, unruliness, waywardness and the irreversible loss of their futures. In fact, most teenagers don't often realise the consequences of their actions until later in life. At that point, it becomes too little too late to regain those lost years and do those things that will help remediate their failures in life.

This is so true because I have experienced this firsthand. Years ago, upon arriving London, UK, as an inquisitive teen, I lived in an area (Peckham) where it was cool to be part of a gang. Perhaps I was influenced more by my curiosity, peer-pressure and the environment than anything else. And to make matters worse, during this period, the theft of personal belongings and intimidation on the streets was common place. Therefore, I had no choice but to join in the action in order to feel safe.

However, had it been that I had a father to provide me with the guidance and security I lacked, the pressures would have been averted. You may ask how I still managed to get out of it all and go about transforming my disadvantaged situation into success. This is something that still surprises me till this day. Perhaps I was simply overwhelmed by the euphoria of leaving behind all the restrictions, punishments and destitution of my former country to finally come to place like the UK, where things were in plentiful supply and, most important, freedom and liberty were finally within my reach. And, in the absence of my lovely mother who was out working most times, it was made all the more easy to do what I wished and when I felt like it.

But a time came when I sat and reflected on life in the UK in comparison to the culture I was used to back in Africa. Indeed, the difference was clear. whilst schooling in Nigeria, I use to be an A grade student at school and the joy of excellence was priceless to me. Now, how come I find myself in the midst of a gang in here in London? Then it suddenly dawned on me that this affiliation would be of no benefit to me. So, I decided to leave the gang losers, and focused more on education.

In the same period, I successfully graduated from college with what I would describe as an 'alright' set of grades in chemistry and physics. Despite the devastation of knowing that I could have done better, I was undeterred and remained resolute. Going to University was a turning point in my life. It completely transformed me and helped in quest to find my identity which was of excellence and greatness. All of which I saw in my father as a child.

Today, you too can reclaim your identity. Are you in a gang, lost, confused, or at a dead end in your life and you see no way out? It is never too late to seek positive transformation and recourse to your identity. Believe me; your identity is within you if only you would take the necessary steps to seek yours today. Perhaps, you do not have both parents in your life. I have been in this situation before and I found solace in knowing that there is a Creator who is the ultimate and compassionate father to all.

I tell you, that your identity holds the key to both break the bondage of failures and to circumvent unforeseen challenges in your journey to attaining a successful, accomplished and fulfilling life.

Below are some steps you can adopt to unlock your true identity, so as lead a purposeful and truly meaningful lifestyle;

*Mentorship*

Identify a mentor; someone who inspires you and that you can look up to. It could be a prominent, a reputable family member, a friend or a public figure. First begin by asking them if they would not mind being your mentor. Otherwise, if your ideal mentor happens to be a public figure that you greatly admire, you need to study and emulate those characteristics you like about them. This is just one way you can begin to develop yourself in all areas for prosperous future.

*Coaching*

Sometimes we feel lost and do not know where to turn for help in various areas of our lives. Coaching is a great way of discerning your identity, but also a way to develop a concrete and clear plan to help achieve your dreams, goals and aspirations. Believe me, if you are a youth, you need coaching, because most times we embark on a course in life without a true understanding of the target we are trying to achieve. Your identity is no different, so if necessary, pay an outstanding coach to help guide you appropriately.

*Discipline and Abstinence*

This is key, particularly if you find yourself in associations of an unhealthy nature. In order to distinguish yourself and be outstanding, you have to learn to distance yourself from certain habits and wrongful addictions. What you watch on TV, the type of music you listen to, and the calibre of friends you keep all influences you a great deal. So, I ask, are you feeding yourself with the right kind of visual entertainment? Do you know the habits and mannerism of your friends? It is up to you to decide. If you are the type who likes smoking, drinking to a stupor and a party animal, then you are setting yourself on a collision course with failure. That is not say that if you do these things you will not be successful. But, whatever you do, do it in moderation. Abstain from all forms of distraction, do not give heed to peer-pressure and create a plan to help you find your identity.

### Self-development, self-believe and, Self-confidence

The number one reason why most young people fail to embrace their identities is that they find it comforting to stand behind other people's shadows. When trying to ascertain your identity, there is need to cultivate the culture of harnessing the inner confidence and belief in your abilities and strengths.

Develop yourself by going to social gatherings which deals with various aspects of personal development, especially, public speaking, writing of books, reading out loud to an audience, identifying hidden skills, and talents, interpersonal skills and more. Try not to focus on your weakness, because you will only end up reverting to your past of conformity, instead of transforming for the better and taking charge.

### Supportive and Positive Influences

The friends and family members that are closest to you, will determine how far you go in life. Whether you like it or not, your choices are influenced by them to an extent. Therefore, it is important to have the right kind of support and influences around you in this journey. Take a look at your friends and family. Is there anyone whose behaviour or character doesn't sit well with you? If so, break away now and embrace those that will help you follow your course. Your identity is imperative, so don't let negativity and confidence dampers deter you.

In summary, my dear friend, it may be that you or someone close to you is displaying behaviour which bears the hallmarks of a lost identity. Don't fret, we can all be transformed and it is never too late. You are more powerful than you may think, so take those steps highlighted above and others you may see fit to aid you in finding the answers you desperately seek today.

If you are teenager, try not to throw away your identity and future by associating with the wrong influences out there. Find a good role model, a life-coach and seek out ways to continually develop yourself so as to unearth the prosperous you. Remember that your ultimate identity is within. I found my identity, so can you today.

# 9

# Step Up And Stand Out

*"Never forget that you are one of a kind. Never forget that if there weren't any need for you in all your uniqueness to be on this earth, you wouldn't be here in the first place. And never forget, no matter how overwhelming life's challenges and problems seem to be, that one person can make a difference in the world. In fact, it is always because of one person that all the changes that matter in the world come about. So be that one person."*

*Richard Buckminster Fuller*

My journey in life has taught me many lessons, most of which are, unfortunately, not part of the general curriculum in schools today. Consequently, I am befuddled that, in the current dispensation, most people seem to believe that they can simply sit in the docks, hide under the guise of their insecurities and allow others to take the front seat and bask in the glory of being under the limelight. Yet most persistently engage in self-pity and repeatedly complain to their friends about the fact that they have not been able to attain and accomplish all those ideas that they have dreamt of and simply do nothing about it. Perhaps if they took the initiative to adopt a different approach to life, then, maybe and just maybe, their stories would change for the better.

Mankind still has a lot to learn from mother nature, because there is a never ending catalogue of animals and vegetation whose survival relies heavily on their unique abilities to differentiate themselves from the crowd. Interestingly, this is demonstrated in the area of competition for food in the food chain, mating partners, during battle for superiority and claiming territories. In other words, the ability of planet earth to sustain our existence is due to its unique resources and properties which sets it apart from the rest of the planetary bodies in existence today.

In a similar fashion, there is need for all humans to get to grips with this poignant reality. This is why I embarked on this journey in order to highlight the imperativeness of differentiating oneself from the pack and inducing success in all facets of our lives. Thus I hereby present to you 'Step Up and Stand Out'. Believe me, this topic has a lot of relevance in my life and the plethora of struggles I have encountered and am stilling overcoming to date. It is a known fact that we all have insecurities, trials and challenges that sometimes seem too much to bear.

Therefore it comes as no surprise to me that many adults and youths who reside in various parts of the world still struggle to extract any true meaning from what is often a life of mediocrity, emulation of the wrong role models and misplaced identities. On the other hand, it will be totally untrue to say that this only applies to the less fortunate and privileged in the society. Absolutely on the contrary, all humans, irrespective of their social and economic standing still experience a variety of difficulties at one point or the other in their lives.

In schools all over the world, especially in the western hemisphere, many teenagers are suffering from dysfunctional identities. This is because a high percentage came from from broken homes, where the mother is left with the herculean and unenviable task of training both the male and female child. Sometimes I wish there were provisions in the national curriculum for people to learn how best to handle the upheavals of life. However, this is not the case and indeed quite unfortunate. Ironically, most people spend so much time learning about a particular area of speciality, but end up graduating without the skill set that is required to handle the challenges that lay ahead.

For me, the early part of my life was not particularly rosy, but, I had nowhere to run to for help with very limited choices available to me. The loss of my father only made matters worse, and my confidence was crushed into pieces. Never did I thought that there would be any light at the end of the tunnel, as they say.

After my ordeal had ended, on Sundays, I was encouraged to attend early morning meetings and would stutter my way through the topics I was given to present to the audience. Sometimes it got so bad that I could not even say my name in front of my friends, not to talk of reciting a sentence from a book.

However, as the years progressed, through school I made new friends, and my situation soon improved. Most important, I was reunited with my brother, which, was one of the happiest days of my life. From that point onwards, it was still a steep, but, smoother journey for both of us.

In the end, I excelled a great deal, because, I had the courage, resilience and mental fortitude to embrace the challenges I was presented with. I was able to transcend from a state of near total dereliction to one of a victor and, stepped up my game in all areas of my life, which made me stand out from the pack.

Beloved, irrespective of what you have experienced in life, do not despair because people will try to dampen your confidence and disregard your personality.

This is simply because they have seen what a bright future you have ahead of you and are simply too intimidated by you. But, always bear in mind that you can recoup your losses by picking up the rubble and rebuild once again. Surely, at first, it may not be easy. But remember to maintain your focus, and be rest assured that it will all be worth the pain and efforts you put in.

In any case, *"pain is short-lived, but, victory is sure, sweet and long-lasting."*

## The Need to Distinguish Yourself and Step Out from the Crowd

This is a question that many people often ask themselves, but, because they are often too comfortable hiding behind the curtains of both misconceived insecurities and in the shadow of those that are deemed to be braver than themselves, they seem not to have any qualms with it. In most situations the will power to change their attitude and approach to stepping out of their pernicious comfort zone has simply been extinguished and is thus nonexistent.

According to Dr Izzo, a doctor of organizational communication, humans are;

*"Like herds of animals at heart." Apparently, "From our early evolutionary history, our instincts tell us it's safest to stay in the pack. Somehow we feel safer doing what everyone else is doing and not sticking our necks out and taking initiative."*

As you can see from the aforementioned statement, all humans are naturally wired to feel comfortable whilst embedded within a crowd of people. Moreover, in other cases, you will find that these people are even more at peace with themselves in situations where the cocoon they find themselves in are with those that their faces are not so foreign to them. This way they become complacent, impenetrably secure and deceptively confident in themselves.

After attending numerous public gatherings, social events and party celebrations, I have come to comprehend this myself, by observing people who, at first glance appear confident and assertive, yet wholeheartedly decline to deliver a simple public address or read an excerpt from book out loud in front of an audience of familiar faces. Believe me, their anxiety is the result of our number one enemy - fear and it is the most prominent factor that has continued to plague people's lives and, as a result, often it is used as an excuse, however valid it may seem.

*As St. Catherine of Siena rightly stated, we should "be who God meant you to be and you will set the world on fire."*

Now, how can you be what God has purposed for, if you don't know how, if you lack total confidence in yourself and are oblivious of the abilities that He has endowed you with? In essence, this is why we need to step up to greatness and stand out of that which we are used to, in order to distinguish ourselves from the pack of people who live in persistent mediocrity, failure and stagnated careers. These category of people I like to refer to as the 'never do, never will, never achieve' and you don't want to find yourself in their company. If you do, you will inevitably be discouraged and, if not careful, get drawn into their folly and pitiful lifestyle.

As I said before, there is need to be mindful of the type of friends you associate with, as this will determine the level of achievements in life. So it is pertinent to learn ways to filter your pool of friends. In fact it is best to have a few useful and forward thinking peers than to have a thousand more that are simply not adding any value to your life. In my life today, there are only a handful of people that I can call friends. Sadly, as I grew up, got wiser and progressed in my career, most of my so called 'friends' that I made at both college and University simply slipped away for reasons best known to them. Nevertheless I was never dismayed, although, it did bother me at the time. But when you possess the maturity to be able to recognise the dynamics of things in life, you come to accept certain attitudes for what they are.

If you are a believer, I say to you that God has a plan for your life and it just so happens that those people who are not supposed to partake in it will eventually fall out of line. In other words as night and day can never collide with each other, so is your purpose with those in your once circle of friends, who, for reasons unknown to you decided to void their once brewing relationship with you. So be not weary. Instead, remain steadfast in your endeavour for greatness and keep your focus firmly on the challenges that lay ahead. In doing so, you will obtain victory, and as they say; "when you have arrived," those same set of individuals who left you because they were intimidated by your drive for success will shamefully return to celebrate with you.

As the American author, William Arthur Ward, rightly stated, that we have to;

*"Do more than belong: participate. Do more than care:*

*help. Do more than believe: practice. Do more than be fair:
be kind. Do more than forgive: forget. Do more than dream:
work."*

Indeed, if you are to achieve a monumental difference in your life, you need to do more than to merely belong. Most prolific complainers are those who have become too accustomed to this notion of belonging to a group. Perhaps not surprising, I know that this may appear impossible and uncomfortable at first. But you should never underestimate the determination you possess on the inside.

Begin by transforming your mindset and emptying all negative beliefs. Ask yourself these three imperative questions; Why am I in this situation? How did I arrive in this situation? And then, what can I do to change it? Afterwards, instead of pondering on the impossible, ignore all those anxious emotions that are clouding your mind right now, and let the true you illuminate out to the world.

All the negative energy that you have stored up on the inside, can make you feel less of a human, but do not quiver. Instead, let your Creator help you to find the answers to those important questions in your mind. Seek him in prayers and He will surely provide you with the 'will power' to overcome all stumblingblocks that are preventing you from achieving your goals, dreams and aspirations. Adopt the mindset of a champion and take bigger and bolder steps to accomplish those desires you seek on the inside. In all, do not look back or wallow in regrets and self-pity. They will only further drag you deeper and deeper, into the pits of losers and non-achievers.

Dear friend, the changes that you seek and yearn for in life can, and, will come to bear, if only you look for ways to accomplish them without contemplating regrets. No one will do them for you, but, yourself. You owe it to your future to make those moves that will get you where your Creator has designed and purposed for you.

Most times we wrongly blame friends, relatives and, so called, 'demons' for the undesirable state of life in which we find ourselves. When in actual fact, we ought to look within and see things the way they truly are. Most people who blame others for their misdemeanours are seemingly oblivious of the true origins of the causes of their problems. Consequently, this has led to the destruction, antagonism and discord seen in many families around the world. Today, we witness brothers wrongly accusing sisters and children accusing parents of being the perpetrator of their demise and poor living standard.

They say that the truth is bitter to accept, but let it be told. We are our own enemy and not other external influences. In some cases, I can comprehend the reasons why some people would want to blame the unseen for their inability to achieve much in life. Because I have seen and experienced the other side of the coin to know too well the tricks that the devil uses to distort our individual and collective welfares.

Paradoxically speaking, if you want to become a banking executive and have no formal education in that specific field, yet you expect to be appointed into a position of such magnitude when the opportunity arises. Think about this for a moment, is this a realistic expectation? I would say no and surely you would share the same sentiment. Because today, many people have become too used to playing the blame card when they have not done their homework beforehand. If you don't do those things that will bring you certain favours in life, then you should not expect to be promoted to a position of prominence. It is simply part of the realities of life and one which we ought to be aware of.

This is the essence of stepping up from the rubble of failures in life. Defy the wrong stereotypes of what people naturally expect from you and step out to obtained greatness. It is said that, *"fortune seeks the brave and not a weakling."* This is so true and one which we must all embrace if we are to be the best we can.

## Rediscovering and Reclaiming the Once Confident You

First take a moment to assess and ask yourself some important questions like, am I happy within myself and the *status quo* in my life? How did I forfeit that once confident me? Is it at all possible to regain and rebuild my once bubbly and outgoing self? and finally, would a renewed confidence open new doors of opportunity for me? If it is you that these question resonates with, then you are perusing the right book.

Sadly, in life, we allow people's perception of us to influence our daily lives and the way we allow ourselves to be perceived by them. This concept of perception is key the type of image, mannerism and attitude we exude. Let's draw a leaf from the mode of life in the jungle and, more specifically, the animal kingdom. The lion has always been seen by both animals and humans alike as the so called 'king of the jungle'. As a consequence, this majestic animal has come to realise this and therefore he often uses it to his advantage. Today we see in many documentaries how lions are able to hunt almost any prey at will with boldness and confidence.

My friend, do you subscribe to the notion that the strength of lions is based on their size and position as the most powerful animal in the jungle? If you believe this to be the case, then you need a swift rethink, as this is a mere fallacy. The rationale behind the unrivalled reputation and notoriety of lions is simply in her belief system and awareness of what others perceive about them. Surely, there are other animals (elephants, hippos, gorilla and grizzly bears, to name a few) with even more imposing presence and a superior capacity to inflict more severe damages on others in its class. But why do lions so often stand out of the pack and for centuries have maintained their reputation as the most revered and feared amongst predators in her class? The answer to this are 'perception and self-belief'.

Most important, it is crucial for you to develop a good image of yourself and not underestimate your capacity to impact change. In my personal life, I have come to understand the usefulness of the aforementioned words. Because the reason for the survival of lions is not their strength or fierceness, but in their superior ability to sense others fear and vulnerabilities and capitalise on them. The same applies to humans. In fact we see this in operation in different areas of our lives, including our place of work, in business and geopolitics.

However, it befuddles me that most people are still oblivious of this important and life changing concept of 'perception'. Because, the latter can change your life for the better and help to you to begin to rediscover the lost confidence you once had in yourself.

Sometimes in life we are too busy with work, business and helping others to fulfil their own dreams, when in reality, we fail in our personal journeys to better ourselves, including; our social and economic standings. As a consequence, most suffer in silence, lead unfulfilled lifestyles and settle for mediocrity. In fact, this can be passed on from generation to generation, because most parents are still failing in their duty to properly equip their children with the necessary skills that they require in order to handle the challenges that lay ahead.

Evidently, in the 'nooks and crannies' of the streets of England UK and other parts of the world today are youths who have lost all hope and suffer misguided identities. Therefore, they are left with no option, but to join various unhealthy groups and involve themselves in all kinds of illicit activities. Then, in their adult years, they discover that they are of no use to the society and most cannot even get decent employment, due to their tarnished history, otherwise known as a 'criminal record' here in the United Kingdom.

Make no mistake, in the absence of an identity, there is no confidence to step out of the crowd, but to simply seek to belong. By doing so, most fall prey to the wrong crowd and leadership.

The issue of confidence is a pertinent aspect of our individual development and weighs heavily on the manner in which we are perceived by our relatives, friends and even those that we barely know. As they say, that, *"first impressions, last longer."*

Moreover, according to the psychologist, Daniel Kahneman,

*"If people are failing, they look inept. If people are succeeding, they look strong and good and competent. That's the 'halo effect.' Your first impression of a thing sets up your subsequent beliefs. If the company looks inept to*

*you, you may assume everything else they do is inept."*

As you can see, it is imperative to project what you want others to perceive about your personality, abilities and way of life. Today, many businesses fail because they have failed to master this concept and look for other excuses to make themselves feel better.

It is not surprising that we don't often praise ourselves and take some credits for the efforts we invest in order to achieve our entrepreneurial endeavours, personal career goals and other areas of our individual lives. Self-praise is another piece of the puzzle in our personal quest to rediscover the confidence to step up and stand out of the crowd.

Recently, I was privileged to meet a young lady who became a friend of mine for only a short period of time. When we meet for the first time, she appeared confident and seemed very engaging. One evening, we arranged to meet at a local pub for some drinks, after work. On arriving at the pub and conversing with her at length, I became aware of her faltering confidence. What really baffled me the most was her persistent rejection of all compliments pertaining to her appearance.

It was so bad that she would not sit in a well lit room and requested that the light be left in the off position. As I probed her further on the reasons for her shattered confidence, it was revealed that she believed that there was nothing pretty or beautiful about her appearance. To compound the issue further, she had issues with trusting others, even when she was being told the truth. In a nutshell, she has allowed people's perception about her to adversely impact her life. Now she finds herself trapped in a cocoon of perpetual isolation and at a perpetual disadvantage.

When I tried to rationalise the origins of this unfortunate notion about herself, it quickly became apparent that it all stemmed from the abuses (verbal defamation, emotional and physical abandonment) she suffered at the hands of her previous male companion. According to her story, her confidence was denigrated the most when she was cheated on by the man she had trusted for so many years.

To compound this further, when confronted with the cheating accusations, he did not deny it, but told her that the reason for his inexcusable behaviour was due to the fact that she was not good enough and too ugly.

This brought an indescribable level of hurt to her and left a

lasting dent on both her personality and image. Her once outgoing and bubbly persona was transformed overnight to one of a reclusive nature. Nowadays, she spends the majority of her time working and at the gym.

According to her, the will to associate with others or get into a new relationship seems all the more daunting. This is just one of the archetypes of how a damaged confidence can affect our lives. Interestingly, there are innumerable examples out there of people who's once brewing confidence has been compromised to the extent that they have lost out on promotions at their place of work, lucrative business deals and lasting friendships.

Beloved, don't let other's perception about you, steal away your shine and chances of ever stepping up to greatness. Step out of the crowd and start living the life and purpose that God has made for you. Believe me, you were uniquely created for a set purpose and not to go to waste. In any case, your perception of yourself is important to your growth and will steer you from the path of failure to one of favour and opportunity.

Some of you may have come from families who are hell-bent on destroying your futures by way of negative impartations in your lives. Instead of caving in and giving up on the race that God Almighty has set before you, it is now time to prove to them that you are made of steel and can go the extra mile to transform your dreams into reality.

In times of grave difficulties and challenges, I learnt the art of mastering perseverance, improvisation and, crucially, the discovery of my God-given purpose. Similarly, today, you too can embark on a journey to rebuild, rediscover and reclaim your ones lost confidence.

Nonetheless, at first, it may seem impossible and unattainable, but with your new found confidence, be wise to embrace boldness, courage and associate with positively-minded and supportive individuals who will encourage you along the way. Then, after it is all said and done, step up to greatness and stand out from the crowd. This is your portion in life and know that you were born with greatness in mind and to be a light to the world.

# 10

# Dreaming Your Way To Monumental Accomplishments

*"Every great accomplishment, begins with an extraordinary dream. But, you must plan, act and believe."*

*Dr Dickson Aleroh*

All human live by their dreams and as a result, we conceive within the corners of our minds a desired place where all the ingredients that will bring a new dimension to our existence can be found. Can you imagine a man with great dreams, but, on the flipside, has not a single achievement to show for it? It is indeed true that we all possess an innate capacity to dream of ideas that are sometimes far beyond the boundaries of our mental domain and imagination.

But, sadly, as the popular adage states , *"all fingers are not equal."* In the same manner, there are and will always be disparities in the content of our individual dreams. No two individuals are ever the same in their social standing, aspirations and accomplishments. This is simply one of the many principles that have continued to govern the human existence and the order of things since the conception of the world.

Take, for instance, two brothers or sisters from the same parents. As they grow up, they naturally begin to develop distinctive and peculiar identities which also encompass their future ambitions, the choices they make and career decisions. While the dream of one of the brothers may be to own a business empire of his own and one which will accord him all the comforts of life, a profession in the musical industry may be the forte of the other.

The same is true for that lady on the other side of the road or that little bright child whose face you wake up to behold daily. The fact is that, though our dreams may vary in its content and magnitude, it does not mean that they are not unique. No one dreams of things other than to enhance his or her life. Otherwise, the essence of dreams would not mean much to your and my life.

## Understanding the Essence Of Dreams

Come to think of it, have you ever pondered on the essence of dreams and why people dream in the first instance? Is there any place for dreams in the 21st century? Are dreams simply a figment of our imagination or are they actually a realistic measure of the heights that we, as humans, are capable of attaining? Are dreams simply a window into the future? Can dreams become reality? Do our dreams affect the choices we make in our daily lives? I am sure that these are some of the array of questions that often get our minds working overtime and thus need to be addressed if we are to obtain anything meaningful from it.

There are innumerable definitions which exist to describe this famous word called, 'dream'. Some describe it as a thought process, an imagination, a series of unrealistic fantasies, or simply a set of desired aspirations and ambitions. Whilst these definitions are not far from the truth, my perception of dream is more akin to a replay of a deeply conceived idea of a place you envision yourself to be in the foreseeable future.

Beloved, the truth of the matter is that our dreams are borne out of a desire for betterment of self and a desperate need for definite changes or a tectonic shift in one's *status quo*. Contrary to some of the definitions above, in my humble opinion, dreams are not common fantasies and illusions of the mind. They are real, relevant and pertinent to the furtherance of those preconceived goals and aspirations we long for in our lives. Because, the moment you stop dreaming, you simply cease to exist to achieve. This is what I refer to as a 'place of lost hope and perpetual discontentment' and it is a point in our lives where those feelings arise which tell you that there is nothing to live for.

Today, many well-meaning individuals have given up on life due to the situation they find themselves in. As a result they have simply given up all hope, thrown in the towel and gone into a state of oblivion. It may be you that I am talking about or perhaps a relative, a friend, or someone close to you. Do you have a dream and have (or foresee) obstacles that have so far hindered your ability to implement that one plan or idea you have conjured for what looks like an eternity now? Fight those demons within which constantly tell you that it is not doable and seek to overpower your will and determination to take those first steps that will put those aspirations in motion.

This leads us to these important questions: what do you dream about? Is it to become, an inventor, a medical practitioner, a PhD holder, a nurse, a successful business owner, an aviation pilot, an engineer, a chief executive of a multinational company, a renowned musical artist, a banker, a public figure, a pastor, an educator, a chef, an Olympic and world class athlete, a fashion designer, an architect, an engineer, a Barrister, or something a little more exotic? Despite the validity of these attainable dreams, it deeply saddens me to realise that many individuals, especially the youths of the present day, are still oblivious of the fact that their dreams will have a strong bearing on the level of their accomplishments and the decisions they make in their various career pursuits and undertakings.

In fact, the notion of dreams makes some people giggle and dismissive at times. Some perceive it as something that you simply think of at night or in your quiet time during the day and then put aside. These people have stopped believing in the strengths and capabilities they have been endowed with and have given up on themselves. Amongst these sets of people are those who consistently underachieve, those that are stagnant in their careers, unfulfilled, unsatisfied, unhappy and complain incessantly about how they are not where they want to be in life. Believe me; you do not want to find yourself in these categories of morons and naive individuals.

There is nothing wrong to be contented with a little. However, if you want to be the envy of the world, get ready to step up and stand out of mediocrity and dream even bigger. In my life this has helped me a great deal. One of my dreams as a child was to become an authority in any field I chose to go into and, many years later, here I am, a PhD holder in the field of Chemistry. Moreover, today I am also a brewing entrepreneur, a public speaker and a transformational coach, which all emanated from a dream. Dreaming is one powerful ability that our Creator has blessed us with so that can have hope and the ability to pry into that which is possible in our lives, only if you identify and follow the purpose of your creation.

## Transforming Your Dreams into Working Success

Dear friend, your dream is like a mirror image of your achievements. In other words, the greater your dreams arc, the bigger your accomplishments would be. They say, *"what the mind can conceive, the body can achieve."* This is one of the secrets to success and it links your dreams to that which you are capable of accomplishing. Now that you know the true importance of dreams, how do you channel and transform them into ideas that will materialise into success for generations to come? Believe me, this is one aspect of life that many have often found wanting.

All dreams involve a sequence of thoughts and this may originate from the activities of the day. Maybe, over the course of your day, you visited an opulent neighbourhood, or, perhaps, you met and conversed with a highly successful school mate of yours who stopped you on the way in his/her Porsche car, or other events that may have triggered some area of need in you. Sometimes, a disappointing relationship, a negative utterance from a supposed friend about your life, a tumultuous childhood experience or other adverse situations, is enough to initiate that vigour within you to want to be found in a better place in your life. If you have experienced any of the above mentioned situations, then you are ready for a transformation.

Without a transformation, dreams are mere 'idle hopes'. Now, how do you transform your dreams into success? This is a question in many people's minds today and their inability to come up with a reasonable answer leads to great anxiety. When Bill Gate (founder of Microsoft) first dropped out of Harvard University, I wonder what his friends would have thought of him. Currently, he is ranked the richest man in the world (2013) and is also the chairman of the company he co-founded (Microsoft). All this was made possible because he had a dream and the will and mechanical drive to transform it into success. In his case, he had the skills and a burning desire to challenge the norm and start his own company which his parents supported wholeheartedly. Therefore, if you have been dreaming about an idea, do not sit on it and wait for others to come and do it for you. It will not happen that way; you need to put in work and have the will and drive to do so.

There are four pillars that will help transform your dreams into lasting success. The first has to do with the actions you take to implement the ideas you dream of. Secondly, how confident you are in those ideas, followed by your assessment of those ideas. Finally, after streamlining your ideas and putting them into motion, are there any successes? Now let us take an in-depth look into the meaning of these four pillars and, hopefully, make them more meaningful to you.

*Action*

When you dream of a big idea, a new career or even a novel business venture, it is very easy to think that you can hit the ground running without considering the challenges involved. Besides that, your willingness to want to take the concrete steps that are required to implement the contents of your dreams is vital to success. Many people have continued to fail in various areas of their lives, simply because they have failed to act on their dreams. Believe me, all they see is the stress and workload involved, so they simply retreat into their cocoon of comfort.

## DREAMING YOUR WAY TO MONUMENTAL ACCOMPLISHMENTS

The youths of today have become directionless, disenfranchised and lacklustre with most stuck with worthless University degrees, because they have refused to act on their God-given purpose. By the way, the latter is revealed through visions and dreams. When we sleep or day-dream, the mind wanders into places of comfort and peace. Sometimes, you envision yourself doing something magnificent in your dreams, but, when you snap out of it, it dawns on you that you are still encapsulated by your daily routine, called 'job'. I say to you, wake up and pursue your dreams and do not waste precious times wallowing in monotony and a dichotomous lifestyle. Your place of happiness is tied to your purpose and when you find yourself doing what you have been called to do, you have then found your purpose. This is your dream(s) in action.

Beloved, I do not know where you are coming from or what your background is like, but, sincerely, I believe that no matter how grand or absurd your dreams are, never allow anybody to discourage you from acting on them. I can assure you that you will surely feel a sense of peace, contentment and happiness within, when you do.

The voice of the enemy will always tell you that your dreams are impossible, and, at the same time, will sow a seed of doubt within to constantly remind you that you need not bother to act at all. In this case, what you say to yourself is important. Naturally, it may already seem unachievable to you, because you have given heed to the voice of discord within. On the contrary, I urge you to ignore the notion of impossibility, forge ahead and dream beyond the confines of your imagination. Most importantly, make that dream a reality by proactive action today.

*Assessment*

Now that you have your big dreams right before your eyes, some of the questions you have to ask yourself at this stage are: what to do with it and how do I go about actualising them? Will my plan impact people's lives? What are my target goals? Who are my target audience, followers, or consumers (all depend on the nature

99

of your ideas)? What are the limitations, risk factors and obstacles that I may encounter along the way? In fact, it is of great importance that you create some quality time to assess the viability of those brilliant ideas that you have dreamt of for so long.

By doing this, your dreams will become more meaningful and, as a consequence, you will begin to view them more objectively. For instance, if your dream is to own a business involving fashion wear. Before starting, you have to think of compiling a sound business plan; consider its location and the sources and amount of finance that may be required. You see, these are some of the areas of assessment that will consume the majority of your time at this stage. However, if done properly, it will help make your vision more real and allay your fears.

Your answers to the aforementioned questions are imperative to carving out a concrete pathway and vision to accomplish your dreams. For example, any dream that will not benefit the life of the common man is bound to fail. If you consider any toothpaste brand out there, it was made to serve a purpose in our daily lives. Without it, we all would have been walking around with bad breathe and unhygienic buccal cavities. As you can see, the success of this type of product is tied to the enhancement of the human lifestyle.

Moreover, you need to know your target audience. In essence, who are your products, invention or business targeting? Is it children, teenagers, adults or those suffering deficiencies in particular areas of their lives. These are factors that can bring a new dimension to your ideas (or dream) if considered.

Most people think that the assessment of an idea is sometimes not necessary. Unbeknown to them that it is a form of planning ahead of time. In actual fact, no business can ever survive in the long term in the absence of a concrete plan. It is akin to piloting a ship blindly without having the necessary training and gear to do so. Remember, that a failure to plan is planning to fail, so assess your ideas before acting on them.

## *Self-believe*

Most people have dreams, but lack the mechanical impetus that will help them take them to a notch up. This is commonly due to the fact that, in the first instance, they do not possess the mental conviction and innate belief in the ideas that they have been so privileged to receive.

Having self-belief is a key ingredient to the successful implementation of any idea and to spur you on to follow your dreams with an unwavering zeal. So, look at yourself in the mirror and say, 'I can do it'. It does not matter how many times you say it, just keep uttering it loudly until it sticks and becomes part of you. Sooner or later, you will discover the belief that you never knew you had within and your confidence will suddenly increase.

Whether you like it or not, your utterances bears great power, so speak positivity always. Unfortunately, this is one area in which most people tend to found wanting and continue to do so. Then they wonder and ponder on the reasons why, despite their best efforts, they have not been able to achieve much in the way of success. So, embrace self-belief and rebuff any residue of doubt, if your dreams are ever going to be actualised. Because, if you do not believe in yourself and in those brilliant ideas you have, then don't expect much in the way of interests from potential external investors.

## *Success*

There is no way that a brilliant idea, if properly implemented (action) and all eventualities considered (assess), will not lead to success. Most prominent business magnates, pioneers and multinational corporations of the day can all attest to this truth. In order to obtain success from your dreams, you need to first consider all the tricks of failure and then translate them into working ideas. This does not imply that you are anticipating the failure, but your awareness of it will help to get all the loose ends in your plan tidied up, so as to prevent it from coming into play.

Remember, you can dream of great things, revolutionary ideas and a better life, just let your imagination run wild. However, what would make those big dreams of yours meaningful is to think and devise ways to bring them into fruition. This is where your mechanical drive and true abilities come into effect. Because, what you do about your dreams today, will determine where you end up tomorrow. In the word of a popular African idiom; *"As you make your bed, so must you lie on it."* So make the wise choice today, because, if you decide to stay idle and hope that a miracle will happen or someone will suddenly emerge from the abyss to do it for you, I'm afraid it will simply not be achieved.

# 11

# Perception: A Deception Of The Mind

*"Let's face it, if you view yourself as a victor, the world will welcome and celebrate you; If you portray yourself as a victim, then you become unwittingly susceptible to predation. It is not that we knowingly want to assume such, but, the way we think and perceive that we are seen by others, often clouds our sense of judgement, reasoning and make us seem inferior to others."*

*Dr Dickson Aleroh*

I can vividly recall some interesting and somewhat laughable events which transpired some years ago, whilst living in small town in Nigeria that remain ingrained in my heart for eternity. Occasionally, in the evenings, I would go out to watch my peers displaying their acrobatic prowess on heaps of fine sand. Although I was intrigued by the sheer bravery and abilities that these young and agile young individuals displayed, the level of skill, difficulty and danger that was involved in the execution of such fascinating feats of human anatomical manoeuvrability did not immediately occur to me. But, as I watched them doing gymnastics, on the inside, I was reassured by the delusion that one day I, too, would be able to do the same. Yes, I know that you think that he must be crazy to conceive such thoughts of embarking on such dangerous plights. But, to me and as with children, I was only exploring my innate adventurous and inquisitive side.

True to my words, as time went by and the days and months grew old, I eventually mustered some much needed courage to take that first step to try similar athletic displays. Notwithstanding my determination, the voice of caution constantly reminded me of the risk I was about to take and, as you can imagine, different thoughts were going through my mind. Although safety was the first point of consideration, I convinced myself that it couldn't be that bad. After all, I have seen it been done many times before, with ease and no complaint of injuries.

In hindsight, I should have been a better student and perhaps, study the techniques involved carefully. Ignoring my worries, I proceeded with the first trial and surprise, surprise! I failed woefully and landed face-down which, as you can imagine, was not so pleasant. In fact, for several days, I was in excruciating pain. All this because I was complacent and had the perception that surely a simple back flip would not be so tricky to execute. After all, those who were doing it were not super humans, but ordinary human beings like me.

Now, irrespective of the fact that I felt like I could do whatever I wanted to (as long as I can conceive it in my mind) and whatever others are capable of doing from a very young age, the notion of risk did not make much sense to me and, as a result, was inconsequential. This is perception in motion and is one attribute that all humans were born with. Because most people are still oblivious of the role that perception plays in our existence, they suffer a great deal.

According to the Oxford dictionary, apparently, in psychology, perception is considered as a series of neurophysiological pathways which also include memory, through which organisms gain an awareness of external stimuli and devise an interpretation of the latter. However, when considering perception, awareness is essential as two categories exist. These are internal and external awareness (or perception). Internal perception is your awareness of something through the senses. In other words, things that you can see, hear or feel. In contrast, external perception pertains more to the way something (or maybe you) is received, comprehended and interpreted by others. The latter could be your friends, spouse or complete strangers.

For instance, pick up a mirror and admire your beautiful features. Can you see it all? I guess not. In fact, provided that you are only looking into one mirror face-on, all you can see is your front-end. However, your rear is completely obscured. Yet, you are reassured that all is well. This is another angle of perception which makes you believe, even in the absence of any physical confirmation. This contradicts the saying, *"seeing is believing."* To me, it is all in the mind and how best you can harness the power therein to your advantage.

Today, on the streets of Great Britain and many parts of the world, there are countless individuals walking with insecurities of differing nature and severity. While some can normally cope with the challenges and side-effects caused by the difficulties they experience, others simply cannot accept that it is part of the price of life and move on. In fact, on a daily basis, they constantly battle with the thoughts of confronting these fears and insecurities. Sadly, many have resulted to committing suicide and incalculable numbers are still living with such unfortunate tendencies, due to the fear that someone somewhere may either discover that they have certain difficulties, then end up being rejected, judged and ostracised.

If this resonates with you, trust me, you are not alone. You can find solace in the knowledge that the problem of insecurity is rife universally. In addition, in most cases, control measures can be easily sought and in others, many remedies are available to help alleviate the effects of whatever you may be experiencing. Crucially, you should know that it is not the end of the world and always have it at the back of your mind that others are living with even worse including physically repulsive imperfections.

Believe it or not, those who are prejudging you for conditions that are sometimes beyond your control are suffering from some type of condition themselves. It is just that in their case it may be hidden and thus not immediately noticeable. But, because they are bent on inflicting pain and sadness on others, they look for an outlet to make themselves feel much better. This way, they feel relieved and return to their little cocoon, called, 'house', and continue to wallow in self-pity. Shamefully, these are the agents of defamation, who go round destroying other's confidence.

I sometimes wonder why a well-meaning human being would want to defame others, just to make themselves feel a sense of worth when they themselves are in a worse state. The fact of the matter is that people need self-assurance and gratification which has always been the case. It's sad, but true. Do not let them get to you, either verbally or otherwise. Always rebuff any destructive criticism and forge on, because, without imperfections, we would not realise our worth in the first instance. Advice is key and self-assurance the more pertinent.

Dear reader, it is imperative to come to a point in your life where you begin to accept who you are and understand the reasons why your Creator, God Almighty has made things the way they are in your life and, crucially, try to develop an impenetrable 'mind of steel'. Because the way you see yourself and your carriage are paramount and if you are not comfortable in your skin, how would you expect others to accept you for who you are. The mind is one of the most powerful tools that often protect our vulnerability to external psychological incursions. For anyone to destabilize your confidence, self-belief and self-worth, they have to prey into the mind. Some are so gifted that they can do this through mere observation of your countenance and general posture. Once, the integrity of mind is compromised, the cracks in your personality are unveiled for the whole world to see.

I once met a young lady, whilst exiting the church premises after the afternoon service. What struck me about her was that she was staring and looking rather puzzled, as if she was lost. So, at a point our eyes met and I asked her if she was alright? Her response was typical. "Yes," she replied. Then I went further, after studying her carefully, by enquiring about her situation. Surprised, she responded like anyone would. How did you know that I was not in that place that I wanted to be in my life right now? My answer to her was short and sweet, "I could simple perceive it, my dear," I said.

Lo and behold, it was indeed true. Suddenly, she began to pour out her heart to me with some troubling details about her life and how she had just returned to church because she had been going through so many ups-and-downs in her life lately. Once again, my instinctive perception of her enabled me to unlock her situation and lack of fulfilment. So, I gave her some encouraging words as was expected of me.

Interestingly, a lot of people would like to be recognised for the right reasons, not due to their insecurities and people's perception. They shy away from stepping up and do not want to stand out for reasons best known to them. Consequently, they resort to forming groups of like minded people and of common interests. That way, within the confines of this group, they feel shielded from external criticisms and thus assume a false sense of security.

But the moment they step out of that place of temporary security and comfort their equilibrium of thought becomes distorted and, as a result, some go into a state of panic and anxiety. At this stage, there seems to be nowhere to hide or anyone to cling onto, as they normally would. This happens because of our failure to peruse and thoroughly understand who we truly are.

A man or woman walking with confidence, despite their insecurities, will command the respect from others because they perceive something unique about them. That thing that others perceive about you, which then attracts them to you, would inevitably overshadow any insecurity you may have. Some would whisper to one another and misconstrue your confidence for arrogance.

Beloved, it is time to begin to change the way you think and confront those demons plaguing your mind. This is not the end of the road for you; rather it is only the beginning of a prosperous journey to a fulfilling lifestyle. In life, the only thing that is constant is change and without it we will not be in existence today. History has proven this to be true. As one generation paves the way for another, so must you let go of the afflictions that people's perception have caused you and begin to unveil a new you today.

## Nurturing the Right Perception About Yourself

We all owe it to ourselves to imbibe all things positive and not leave room for vulnerability to external influences which can hamper all our efforts to overcome adverse perceptions. The latter may be by way of antagonistic statements, secret gossips and unwarranted criticism. Indeed, as humans, we sometimes hate pre-judgement of any kind, even if the content therein might have some remnant of truth. No wonder why the wise man would say that, "*the truth is bitter to swallow.*" Surely, if we learn to exude those desired qualities that we want others to see in us, then and, only then, shall they begin to look and think of us in both a positive and favourable fashion.

In your quest to stem the tide of regressive statements, a good place to begin may be by accessing the nature of those comments and invest some quality time in identifying and building up your strengths, abilities and talents, without considering any limitations. Certainly, no man was created with the latter. Moreover, when approached by strangers or perhaps an old school friend, do not assume an inferior position, because you see that they drive a nicer car, live in a better house and own a successful business. This may put you in a disadvantageous position. Thus it is pertinent to develop a mind of steel and one that responds favourably to change, in order to help reclaim some lost ground in your once diminished confidence and *status quo*. You cannot live a pretentious life, but one of fulfilment and visible progress.

To that end, self-belief is also vital, because, without it, we are like a buoyant ship with holes, waiting to sink at a moment's notice. No wonder why many youths of the present day are jobless and without any defined goals in their brewing lives. So they hover to and fro, seeking for comfort and safety in the wrong places and seeking out sorrowful rationalistic point of view(s), so as to aid the justification of their recalcitrant behaviours in the society which they reside.

In contrast, when adulthood sets in, the dynamics of our lives changes and so does the nature of our insecurities and expectations from our families and friends. In all, do not allow the pressures of the opinions of enemies deter you from forging ahead to achieving those burning desires you have dreamt of for so long. Rather, you need to get to a place where you begin to foster the culture of self-praise, self-assuredness and getting to know your worth. Because no other person can intricately comprehend the state of affairs within you like yourself.

Irrespective of what you may have been told in the past, you can be the best in all areas of your life and accomplish anything. The voice of the enemy cannot break you, if you are determined, persevere and hold on to the words that God Almighty has said concerning your life, that you will dominate, overcome and increase (success, fulfilment and happiness). In fact, the voice of the enemy is not difficult to discern, because anyone can be used to speak negativity into your life.

Others will stereotype you based on your race, accent and social standing. After all, the generations before you also suffered the same faith and have done for centuries. So why listen and leave your precious mind vulnerable to be infiltrated by such. Some will say who are you to want to dream big? How dare you even try to start that new business or career that will get you to a higher level? What experience do you have in running anything that qualifies you and justifies you being given such magnanimous responsibility at your place of work? Are you really as good as others say you are? Who are you to become the CEO of this multinational organisation? This is the voice of doubt which can only come from one source, the 'enemy' within, or even from external sources.

Remember that if you are comfortable within yourself, no word defamation can permeate through the walls of defences that you have built to safeguard your progress in life. As it is written in the Holy Scriptures (Jeremiah 29.11; NIV), *"For I know the plans I have for you, declares the Lord, plans to better you and not harm you, plans to give you hope and a future."* So, as you can see, your Creator did not create you so that you can wallow in penury and live in fear of what others might say about you. Completely the contrary, it is to better that you prosper and above all keep safe at all times and in all your endeavours.

So, what have you got to lose, nothing. If anything, those who are busy criticising and gossiping about you barely have enough time to invest in their own progress. Why? Because they spend so much of it exploring all avenues to take others into the pit of failure they have dug for themselves. This is the number one reason why many people today have resulted to substance abuse and, eventually, end up in psychiatric hospitals, because, they see no way out of their situations.

In spite of the nature and severity of what you may be going through, always find solace in the fact that, *"where there is a problem, there is always a solution."* Seeing that there is no smoke without fire, by identifying the origins of your problems or the reasons why you feel a certain way about yourself, you are on track to finding the solution to the issues and challenges that you are facing.

Need I say more? Beloved, having a positive outlook about yourself (internal perception) is crucial to staving off external incursions on your overall person. Besides the above, develop the culture of adaptation and transformation. As the saying goes, *"call a spade, a spade."* In other words, it is what you show to the world that they would use to describe you. Now search within, ask yourself if what you are portraying is what you want others to see in you? Or could you amend or transform your ways and take on the positives from these comments that you are getting from your well-meaning friends and relatives? The ball is in your court, so make the right judgement about yourself and do that which will edify you for a better future.

In all, having the right perception about yourself will change your world and bring a new wave of opportunities, friends and success your way. As much as God Almighty wants you to excel, He also requires you to put in the work needed to get you to your place of fulfilment and peace. Trust me, if you follow His ways and apply the tenets of His teachings, as are carefully laid out in the scriptures, you will never go wrong. You are winner and a conqueror, but you need to believe and accept that you are, before it can begin to manifest in your life.

## The Advantages of Fostering the Right Perception

If there is one book that has been of great inspiration to me, it is the Holy Scriptures, which is far beyond the ordinary. In Hosea 4:6, God Almighty, through His prophet, highlighted the fact that, *"people do perish due to the lack of knowledge (or vision)."* While it is sometimes true that, *'what you don't know won't kill you.'* But, if you do know, but refuse to apply it or comply, it will surely bring great harm to you. What the scriptures states is so true. In fact, it applies to all areas of our lives and 'perception' is not exempt.

Having and nurturing the right perception is crucial to our survival. Besides, how about using the perception of others about you to your advantage or to outwit them? Do you know that you are gifted with the ability to sense what others are thinking? Can you reverse those thoughts and stop being dampened when judged wrongly? How can negative perception favour you? These are just some of the many questions on our ever inquiring minds that formed the basis of the preceding sections. So, why not sit back, relax and follow me as I take you on a journey to unlocking the power you did not realise was within you. That is the power of discernment.

Quite often, we are criticised, misunderstood and wrongly judged, for one reason or another. Maybe you have a unique appearance, dress differently, speak with difficulty or excessively, or have a certain uncontrollable condition, that others usually take note of because it is deemed too offensive. Now ask yourself these questions: why do I feel this way, that others are always taking note of my insecurities? Could it be that my thoughts are inclined towards certain misconceptions about myself? Or could they simply be thinking of what I am perceiving about themselves? Are my peers really talking about me after a meet-up? If you are of this mindset, then you need to delete from you mind such self-critical thoughts and transform your thought process. Because there is power in change.

Frankly, when people see an imbecile walking on the street,

most will immediately prejudge the situation out of their own stupidity, which is completely natural. But if they could stand back and try to get to know the individual, both inwardly and not merely based on appearance, they will find that there is something unique about them. Often they may discover them to be even more special than they themselves. Negative perception is ignorance and foolishness. And it is quite surprising that too many people still engage in it today. In some cases, you will find out that if an individual is low in self-esteem, he or she would automatically seek to make others feel the same way. No more! Say no to defamatory sentiments and evil intents. Believe me; God Almighty has fortified you with the nutrients that are required to guard against negative perceptions.

Today, you too can pick up the rubble of your already shattered personality and begin to rebuild your confidence right now. Next time, if someone says to you that you do not appear confident or that there may be something wrong with you in any way, shape or form, you owe it to yourself to quickly rebuff it and do not let it register in your mind. This is the essence of having a mind of steel, an impenetrable shield to adverse comments and remarks of sadists. Tell them to walk on with their insecure selves, so you do not revert back to what you use to be. But you must do this in a humble and diplomatic manner. Remember that you owe it to yourself to confront certain adverse perceptions, if you hope to reclaim your once lost happiness.

When it comes to the issue of confidence building and rebuffing negative perceptions, I am not a stranger to it. For many years, I battled with speech difficulties which, on many occasions, prevented me from engaging in social events and speaking tasks in a public setting. Sometimes it got so bad that I would not want to read a book or answer phone calls in front of my friends or even strangers. Things got so bad that, when asked to give a presentation, I would stutter all the way and sometimes it was as if I was about to be mauled by a pack of vicious dogs. Believe me, if I could have died, I would have taking that option instead of allow myself the shame of staring at people who probably thought that I would falter at any given moment. Beloved, this plagued my life for a long time and almost made me a recluse to the outside world.

The experiences were sometimes unbearable and I would often beat myself up about it. Despite all that I had gone through in my young life and the abuses I faced in the hands of relatives, I pulled through and turned it into an advantage in my life. On many occasions, I would sense people talking about my difficulty in speaking, but, although it sometimes bothered me, I forged on and, as result, my determination to overcome it got even stronger. Whenever I was presented with the opportunity to speak, I would volunteer to do it. Soon, people began to sense the resurgence of the confidence in me. Since I began speaking, the satisfaction that is received after hearing the listeners comments, brought about a feeling that is better than winning a truck-load of gold. It is simply priceless.

Fighting negative perceptions is like an uphill battle that many people, unfortunately, have to contend with on a daily basis and if you are not equipped with the right knowledge to tackle it, you are at an undeserved disadvantage in the society we live in today. Very often, I observe pastors, politicians and presenters, on television, speaking eloquently about different subject matter and issues that affect us all. However, I am struck and impressed by the manner in which they skilfully execute their speeches. The President of the United States of America, Barack Obama, in particular. He has been such an indispensable inspiration to many, myself included.

When I decided to start speaking in public settings, I made it a point of duty to attend the Toastmasters International Speaking Club here in City of London, UK. It was during this period that I began to listen to both experienced and amateur speakers, observed their body language and perused the different ways of speaking. It was at this point that I discovered that speaking is an art in its own right. Truly, my eyes were opened to world of public speaking and the sheer number of individuals who were dealing with the same issues that I was going through, thinking that I was alone in my battles. In fact, the number one factor that kept coming up was the, 'glossophobia' (fear of public speaking). It was as if, a 'Pandora box of knowledge' was suddenly opened and it all became clear to me, that all humans have one insecurity or the other.

In actual fact, we constantly battle with ourselves, either, secretly, by way of medication or therapy or by other avenues. So, as I studied the different speech patterns and the dos and don'ts, it dawned on me that the issues that I had battled with since my childhood could really be defeated. But it necessitated hard work, perseverance and an unwavering will. Then I mustered some courage, boldness and bravery to grab the bull by the horns and walk with my head high on the path to revivify my confidence in public oratory.

Sincerely, from here onwards, for the simple fact that I came to the knowledge that people's perception about me is borne out of their own deep seated phobias, that they themselves are too reluctant to work on, I could now look straight into the audience's eyes while speaking and not be perturbed at all. It is reassuring, even if my delivery was not going to be wholly perfect at all times. Thankfully, I find solace in the knowledge that I can do all things through Jesus Christ who strengthens me and if I can do it, so can you. Beloved, there is no mountain too high, that you cannot conquer. All you need do is to make your mind up this moment and take that first, and sometimes, difficult step to achieve those dreams that are yet to be transformed into active success.

As the wise man would say, *"fortune seeks the brave and not a weakling."* This is one very powerful quote that I embrace when those demonic insecurities tries to infiltrate my mind, so as to slow down my progress in my quest to accomplish those goals that I deeply desire. So far, I have never had any regrets, but a feeling of satisfaction whenever I ignore those negative voices within me and take a big step in my life. More so, that people who used to know me would look at me and marvel, because they thought that I was going to just sit in ruins and take the beating, due to the wrongful perception that people were thinking of me in a certain way. In life, if you want to achieve anything of great significance, you need not be weary, but embrace who you are and let your imperfections perfect you. In life, what is crucial is not the quantity of resources that you are given that matters, but what you are able to achieve from the little that is available to you.

By knowing what others think about you or what they are experiencing is a powerful tool that you could utilise to your advantage. This is one secret that you need to know about human-to-human interaction. When you meet an individual for the first time, they immediately begin to unravel your personality, your mannerism and make observations about your style of dressing, how you smell, talk, smile, your posture and body language. By doing this, they come to different conclusions about you. Now, the onus is on you to turn those conclusions or perceptions, however right or wrong they may be, around and begin to shine today.

## Six Keys to Attract Positive Perceptions

This section would not be complete without some tangible and practical ways to attract favourable perceptions and compliments from others. Here are some pointers to help you in your desire for improvements in the way you are perceived by both yourself and others.

### Image is everything

Do you recall the first time you tried on a sophisticated suit or that luxurious dress that you purchased from your favourite boutique, with a brand new shoe to match and took a peep in the mirror? Remember how you felt? I trust that the feeling must have been refreshing, of admiration and one of great liking for yourself. In fact, when I tried on mine for the first time, I couldn't believe how transformative it was. I felt like a business mogul, it was simply exhilarating.

This is exactly the reaction of others when they see you outside, in the streets, at your place of work, or at a function. However, you may not have realised this, but, as soon as you leave your home, you become vulnerable to people's judgement, seeing that the mirror you so much lean on is no longer in hand to reassure you that all is well with how you look. Therefore, it is important to properly and carefully groom yourself, so that you can walk confidently. This way you attract the right kind of criticism and compliment.

Furthermore, this also applies to your home. As the saying goes, *"charity begins at home."* In essence, if you are dirty at home, it will reflect on not only in the way you look, but in the way you do things and certain traits you display. A clumsy person at home will always do the same wherever they visit, even at their place of work. When I started working at a small-to-medium size enterprise in the East Midlands of the United Kingdom, many commendations were dished out to me by my manager at the time. This was because the office and work areas were always clean and clutter-free. Thus I commanded a lot of respect from him for that single gesture. It was not as if I felt that I wanted him to be impressed by my cleanliness. On the contrary, I was just doing that which comes natural to me.

Having the right image breeds commonality and cohesion between two likeminded people. In my life, I have been privileged to meet a lot of people who claim to be one thing or the other. But trying to get an invite to see them at their abode is something else. In most cases, you will get a gentle refusal. If you look deeply, 9 out of 10 times it is because they are ill-prepared. In other words, their homes are not presentable, to put it lightly.

On a particular occasion, I met a gentleman from Sierra Leone who once told me that he cannot have a relationship with anyone who is clumsy and does not know how to tidy up their immediate environment. Truthfully, upon visiting his residence, it was indeed very presentable and correlated with his ethos. Therefore, I am of the school of thought that image is indeed everything. If you project the right image about yourself, then the result is attraction of positive compliments and good perception.

*Attitude*

According to J. J. Wong, *"A bad attitude is like a flat tyre, if you don't change it, you will never go anywhere."* In anything you do, your attitude has to be right if you hope to progress to the next level. No one likes to associate with a person of truculent behaviour, temperament and irrationality. Because the way we treat others, how we relate to them, our behaviour towards others and the reception they are given, hinges a lot on how we are perceived by them. Sincerely, it helps to better our image and positions us in a more positive light to receive favours from unexpected sources. If your attitude is that of cohesion, compassion and consideration, then people will easily warm up to you. Therefore, having the right attitude is of great importance to your progress in life and determines the types of associations you attract.

Could you imagine being in a house with an insolent, argumentative and uncompromising partner? Do you feel like being around them all the time? Surely not. In fact, people with faulty attitudes often end up in isolation, with no one to call friend. Simply because they display the wrong attitude which others could not put up with. Today, too many relationships have collapsed, partly due to this issue of attitude defect. In addition, your colleagues at work would resent you and eventually drift way, if your attitude is not up to par with expected standards. Simple gestures, such as a welcoming smile and a hand shake, can make your interaction with others more fruitful. In a nutshell, in life, attitude plays a pivotal role.

*Exude confidence*

Confidence is highly attractive, as I have experienced over the years. Very often I come across people who appear confident on the outside, while, on the inside it is an entirely different matter. Even myself, I struggled with confidence deficiency, due to the way in which I was brought up as a child. This affected me greatly and the kind of friendships that I was able to form. However, based on the knowledge that I have gained in relation to the perception, this is no longer an issue.

If you look around you, there are people who carry daily burdens of insecurity with them, without displaying any visible signs to show that they are indeed suffering from one thing or another. But, by digging deeper, their struggles will become all the more apparent. Lack of confidence can impinge your ability to approach others and vice versa. Thus, if you want to appeal to more clients in your business, people at your place of work, or a new partner, it is high time to take that first step to build your confidence. Those who walk, speak and behave with some self-assuredness often go very far in all areas of their lives. Especially when it pertains to promotion at work and appointments.

*Accept who you are*

The one thing that you cannot change in life is who you are, because God Almighty has created you that way. However, you can always change how you act, react and approach situations. Many times we see people say that I wish I could change one feature or another on my body. By doing so, they hope to gain more acceptance and validation from friends, family, or someone of interest that they have been trying to attract for so long with very little success. This is a myth that most have been led to believe will change their lives and the way they are viewed and received by others.

On the contrary, people like when you are original and true to yourself. Because, if you are true to yourself, you will accept who you are and be comfortable in your own skin. A confident man or woman need no validation. Therefore, he or she finds consolation in knowing that they are who they are and nothing can better the attributes, talents and beauty that they have been endowed with so graciously, by God Almighty, and what they have come to know as the truth about themselves.

Essentially, when you have accepted who you are, you find peace and no one can tell you otherwise. At the end of the day, what have you got to lose by being youself? Many have gone under the knife so that they can be accepted by society, only to find out that the outcome was a lot worse than they had bargained for. So they spend almost all their savings on painful reconstructive procedures which only worsen their situation. Beloved, what I am trying to convey to you is that you should celebrate your looks, your gifts and who you are, because you are unique in all aspects. Just like your fingerprints, no two person's are the same. In the same light, we were all created differently and with peculiar characteristics. By knowing and accepting who you are, others will follow suit.

*Cleanliness*

When I think of the concept of cleanliness, words such as purity, welcoming and appeasing immediately come to mind. No wonder that they say, *"cleanliness is next to Godliness."* As a child, when I first entered the United Kingdom, I was amazed at the look of the streets. At the close of day, I often observe cleaners, equipped with industrial vacuum cleaners, going to and fro, vacuuming every traceable piece of cabbage on the roads and street corners. Unlike where I came from, at the time, where the streets were not so delicately cared for. Although my parents and extended family did instil in me the need to lead a neat and presentable lifestyle. Every morning, before making the long walk to school, I would ensure that the house was spotless. Then, as an adult, I came to comprehend the imperativeness of cleanliness.

Furthermore, the wow factor makes me happy and people are impressed by tidiness. Sometimes, I ask myself, why do people always want to look their best on the outside, yet they cannot maintain their immediate surroundings? Perhaps laziness is one factor to be blamed, or could it be that most are simply too complacent when behind closed doors. After all, no one is looking. You may think that your activities are not being checked by anybody, but what about your children, if you have some, or even your husband, wife or partner? Do you care enough to know what their opinion about you may be? If it is negative, then you have a lot of improvements still to implement in your chaotic life. If you won't eat in a dirty restaurant, or go on a date in filthy clothing, why should others tolerate such from you? This is worth a thought and it might surprise you how different the nature of your interactions and associations may become.

*Knowing your onions*

We all have a career, but are you well-grounded in your area of expertise? Or are you just one of the staff members who is too busy trying to conform, instead of exhibiting those qualities that will make you stand out of the pack? As Pablo Picasso orated in one of his thinking moments, *"When I was a child my mother said to me, 'If you become a soldier, you'll be a general. If you become a monk, you'll be the pope.' Instead I became a painter and wound up as Picasso."* How amazing it is for one to realise that there is a genius within, at such a young age. As you would agree with me, Picasso is undoubtedly one of the most renowned painters of all time, with most of his works commanding millions of dollars at auctions around the world.

Sad, but true, most people like associating with the best kid on the block. If you are good at what you do, then you will become an overnight celebrity. Because of this, people will immediately gravitate towards you. Though this might be driven by their curiosity to want to affirm if what others have been saying about you is indeed true. If you consider the case of Mohammad Ali, as a charismatic boxer he was excellent at his trade and more so, he displayed certain ingenuity that made him a living legend in the boxing arena, as the 'greatest' heavy weight boxer'. Therefore, by diligently studying and perfecting his craft, he stood with presidents, prime ministers, kings and queens. You can do the same today, by tightening those loose screws in your area of speciality and begin to receive recognition for your works.

*Appreciate life and People*

Sometimes, life can be tricky, not the least the stresses and burdens it thrusts on us. Too often, many people have become accustomed to complaining and blaming their failures or inability to achieve anything of significance on one thing or another. This has made so many of them grumpy and filled with anger and resentment. But how about trying a different take on life itself? Is your position that bad, that you cannot at least be thankful to God Almighty for all that you have accomplished so far? Sometimes we allow our minds to be preoccupied with the bigger picture, whilst ignoring those little, but, often significant victories we attain, unknowingly.

The moment we begin to appreciate life a lot more, there lies the inception of true happiness. Because, whether you like it or not, as long as night and day exist, so will there be both good and bad moments. So, I ask, why wallow in temporal pain, when you can enjoy life a lot more? In short, others can sense your body language when you are going through difficult moments, even when you maybe don't realised it yourself. Remember that you are what you attract. If you are happy, you will attract happiness and people of similar state of mind. Sadness will always cloud your thoughts and prevent you from seeing the true essence of life.

Look around you and you will soon see that there is more to your existence than it seems. Believe me; nobody wants to be around bitterness, self-pity and lowliness. So stop and start appreciating life for what it is and, in doing so, you will learn to accommodate other's shortcomings. Always be that person you want to see in others and you will be a winner of many hearts and minds.

Beloved, these six keys have been given as only a guide. There are numerous ideas out there that you can apply in order to better yourself and get noticed for the right reasons. However, in your stride for betterment, know that perception plays a fundamental role in our lives as humans and you can use this concept to your advantage for good.